THE TECH SET

Series Editor
ELLYSSA KROSKI

2

Mobile Technology and Libraries

JASON GRIFFEY

facet publishing

© Jason Griffey 2010

Published by Facet Publishing,
7 Ridgmount Street, London WC1E 7AE
www.facetpublishing.co.uk

Facet Publishing is wholly owned by CILIP: the Chartered Institute of
Library and Information Professionals.

First published in the USA by Neal-Schuman Publishers, Inc., 2010.
This UK edition 2010.

British Library Cataloguing in Publication Data
A catalogue record for this book is available from the British Library.

ISBN 978-1-85604-722-7

Printed and bound in the United States of America.

To the ever-patient Dr. Betsy Sandlin;
my wife, my love, and my best friend

CONTENTS

Don't miss this book's companion wiki and podcast!

Turn the page for details.

THE TECH SET is more than the book you're holding!

All 10 titles in THE TECH SET series feature three components:

1. the book you're now holding;
2. companion wikis to provide even more details on the topic and keep our coverage of this topic up-to-date; and
3. author podcasts that will extend your knowledge and let you get to know the author even better.

The companion wikis and podcasts can be found at:

techset.wetpaint.com

At **techset.wetpaint.com** you'll be able to go far beyond the printed pages you're now holding and:

- ▶ access regular updates from each author that are packed with new advice and recommended resources;
- ▶ use the wiki's forum to interact, ask questions, and share advice with the authors and your LIS peers; and
- ▶ hear these gurus' own words when you listen to THE TECH SET podcasts.

To receive regular updates about TECH SET technologies and authors, sign up for THE TECH SET Facebook page (**facebook.com/nealschumanpub**) and Twitter (**twitter.com/nealschumanpub**).

For more information on THE TECH SET series and the individual titles, visit **www.neal-schuman.com/techset**.

FOREWORD

Welcome to volume 2 of The Tech Set.

Today's library patrons are untethered and free of the limitations of the desktop computer; they are accessing information from a variety of devices, including cell phones, PDAs, laptops, and e-book readers. In *Mobile Technology and Libraries,* author Jason Griffey explains how to provide cutting-edge mobile library services to patrons everywhere. This top-notch primer provides a comprehensive view of the mobile Web landscape and outlines how to establish a mobile Web presence for your library. Whether you are hoping to create portable instructional resources, offer on-the-go library tours, create a mobile Web site and catalog, or offer SMS text reference and notifications, you will find out how in this guidebook.

The idea for The Tech Set book series developed because I perceived a need for a set of practical guidebooks for using today's cutting-edge technologies specifically within libraries. When I give talks and teach courses, what I hear most from librarians who are interested in implementing these new tools in their organizations are questions on how exactly to go about doing it. A lot has been written about the benefits of these new 2.0 social media tools, and at this point librarians are intrigued but they oftentimes don't know where to start.

I envisioned a series of books that would offer accessible, practical information and would encapsulate the spirit of a 23 Things program but go a step further—to teach librarians not only how to use these programs as individual users but also how to plan and implement particular types of library services using them. I thought it was important to discuss the entire life cycle of these initiatives, including everything from what it takes to plan, strategize, and gain buy-in, to how to develop and implement, to how to market and measure the success of these projects. I also wanted them to incorporate a broad range of project ideas and instructions.

Each of the ten books in The Tech Set series was written with this format in mind. Throughout the series, the "Implementation" chapters, chock-full of detailed project instructions, will be of major interest to all readers. These chapters start off with a basic "recipe" for how to effectively use the technology in a library, and then build on that foundation to offer more and more advanced project ideas. I believe that readers of all levels of expertise will find something useful here as the proposed projects and initiatives run the gamut from the basic to the cutting-edge.

Jason Griffey has been writing and speaking about Web 2.0 and mobile technologies in libraries for many years and has served as the Chair of BIGWIG, the social software interest group of LITA, since 2005. I knew that Jason would excel at writing a practical guide to mobile technology for librarians and he didn't disappoint—in fact just the opposite. Jason put together a first-rate guide to all-things mobile for librarians. Get ready to *wow!* patrons with your mobile offerings after reading this book.

Ellyssa Kroski
Information Services Technologist
Barnard College Library
www.ellyssakroski.com
http://oedb.org/blogs/ilibrarian
ellyssakroski@yahoo.com

Ellyssa Kroski is an Information Services Technologist at Barnard College as well as a writer, educator, and international conference speaker. She is an adjunct faculty member at Long Island University, Pratt Institute, and San Jose State University where she teaches LIS students about emerging technologies. Her book *Web 2.0 for Librarians and Information Professionals* was published in February 2008, and she is the creator and Series Editor for The Tech Set 10-volume book series. She blogs at iLibrarian and writes a column called "Stacking the Tech" for *Library Journal*'s Academic Newswire.

PREFACE

Today, worldwide mobile telephone subscriptions are at 3.3 billion—equivalent to half the global population.[1] In over 50 countries, cell phone penetration (the number of cell phones per person) has climbed above 100 percent, and by 2010, 90 percent of the world's population will have access to a cell phone signal.[2] These statistics are irrefutable evidence of a major shift in the way that people everywhere interact with information. They also foretell the next real paradigm shift in ways people—and libraries—will gather, use, and share information.

As phones become more data-capable, fewer people need a computer to connect with their infosphere. Instead, they use a cell phone as their primary interface for surfing the Web, listening to music, watching television, reading books, and communicating with friends. The mobile phone has become, over the past ten years, one of the major interfaces people use to access and share information. Librarians need to be aware of these changes, peer forward, and prepare for the future of library mobile interaction.

▶ ORGANIZATION AND AUDIENCE

Mobile Technology and Libraries is designed to help librarians develop a mobile library Web site, use Short Message Services (SMS) communication, and reach library patrons in a new and exciting way. This book is aimed not only at librarians just beginning to step foot into the mobile environment but also speaks to the various functional parts of the library, demonstrating places in public services that mobile technology is applicable, as well as providing the recipe (including code samples and other technical information) for the production of services used by information technology librarians. At the conclusion of this book, librarians of all types will be able to launch their libraries into the mobile realm.

Chapter 1 begins with an introduction of mobile technology in libraries and a discussion of the major and minor platforms, cell phone types, and other mobile-related services. Chapter 2 covers everything you need to plan for integrating mobile technology into your library's services, including which situations are appropriate for mobile technology use and the different services available. Chapter 3 covers how to implement a mobile technology plan. Chapter 4 covers mobile services marketing techniques. Chapter 5 covers general best practices, while Chapter 6 covers measuring the success of your library's mobile services and how to build off your successes.

Mobile Technology and Libraries is designed to help put librarians in all types of settings ahead of the technology curve and integrate the mobile movement into their everyday services.

▶ NOTES

1. Reuters. Available: www.reuters.com/article/technologyNews/idUSL2917209520071129 (accessed November 18, 2009).

2. GSM Association. 2006. "Universal Access Report." Available: www.gsmworld.com/documents/universal_access_full_report.pdf (accessed November 18, 2009).

ACKNOWLEDGMENTS

I owe a debt of gratitude to more people than I have room to name, but I would like to especially thank the following:

Endless gratitude goes to my colleagues at the University of Tennessee at Chattanooga, especially Dean Theresa Liedtka and our ever-amazing Head of Reference and Instruction, Virginia Cairns. Both of you put up with my rambling and crazy ideas more than perhaps you should. Also thanks to Mike Bell, my somewhat curmudgeonly mentor, and the members of the IT department, Andrea Schurr, Chris Ryan, and Stephen Leather. Thanks for keeping the place running!

Thanks to my extended librarian family on Twitter, FriendFeed, and the rest of the social Web. You guys keep me interested in this stuff and inspire me. I'd list you all, but I'd need another 50 pages. Special thanks, though, to Toby Greenwalt and the tech group at the Skokie Public Library for being willing to share their code with me.

Thanks, finally, to my family, especially my daughter, Eliza, who is far too young to be putting up with Daddy's writing but does so anyway.

▶1

INTRODUCTION: MOBILE TECHNOLOGY BASICS

- ▶ Overview and Examples
- ▶ Importance to Libraries
- ▶ Platforms

▶ OVERVIEW AND EXAMPLES

Librarians have long been avid users of technology, blazing many trails in the early days of what was then called "automation." Over the past 40 years technology has marched closer and closer to the user, having moved from mainframes that were accessed via terminals to shared "personal" computers, to the current computer-on-every-desk. This march is continuing but in a slightly new way. The newest revolution in computing isn't taking place on anything that most librarians would even call a computer. The new computer revolution is taking place in your pocket.

Technology in general and computers specifically have long been moving toward mobility as well. Some librarians will remember the first laptops, described as truly "portable" computers in the same way that your current desktop PC is portable, if you chose to lug it around. Modern laptops are small, nimble, and highly portable, but nothing comes close to the mobility inherent in the mobile phone. Not only does the form factor of the cellular phone lend itself to the ultimate in portability, pocketability, the move toward the consolidation of multiple features in the modern cell phone means that you can increasingly use the phone for things that you once needed to carry a separate device to accomplish. New phones not only make calls but they also play music, show video, tell you where you are via GPS (global positioning system), and browse the Web.

These phones have become, for users, an information hub. They consume media and in turn create media using the devices. Cell phones have changed journalism, because everyone is now a photographer and at a moment's notice can capture events in nearly real time. They provide entertainment in the form of music, television, movies, and games. They read audiobooks to patrons, and patrons read the newspaper on them.

This mobile phone is the topic of this book. As we in libraries move toward more and more patron-focused services, we will need to understand and exploit this new class of computing device. The key reason that mobile phones are changing the face of information interaction isn't their ability to consume the media mentioned; it is their connectivity. The ability to be constantly connected to the Internet is truly revolutionary, and the changes this connectivity brings to the library world are only now beginning to show themselves.

Libraries have, over the past five years, focused heavily on providing digital services, especially reference services, via mobile channels. Libraries these days are providing reference via phone, chat, Facebook, and more and more via services that are specific to mobile phones like Simple Message Service, or SMS. The potential for these services is growing daily as well, with new phones adding functionality with every new release. Why should libraries be focusing on mobile technology, especially with all of the other demands we deal with daily?

To quote William Gibson, "the future is here, it's just not evenly distributed." If we want to see what libraries will be dealing with in the mobile realm, it would be wise for us to look at the rest of the world and notice that mobile phones are becoming the primary information interface for users everywhere. At the time of this writing, at least 3.3 billion people in the world use cell phones, according to Reuters. In over 50 countries, cell phone penetration (the number of cell phones per person) is above 100 percent. In 2010, 90 percent of the world's population will have access to a cell phone signal. It is the fastest growing, most embedded, and most widely adopted technology in existence today.

And it's not just simple numbers; it's also usage. In Japan, users of mobile devices are reading and writing novels on them. One of the bestselling novels in 2007 in Japan was written on a cell phone and largely read there. One of the most popular applications on the Apple iPhone is Stanza, an application that allows users to download and read public domain classics. Another is the *New York Times* application, which reformats the Gray Lady into something that is consumable on a three-inch screen. These mobile applications are just the tip of the impending iceberg, and the iPhone is just the first of the new super-phones that are much closer to computers than anything that has come before. The general movement in the development of mobile phones is toward what are currently called "smartphones." These phones include the ability to e-mail, calendar, browse the Web, and more from your phone, effectively marrying the PDA and the phone into a single unit. Some, such as the iPhone, also work as media players, handling audio and video files for on-the-go listening/watching.

Over the next two to five years, we will see an explosion of fully featured smartphones that will make the iPhone look primitive by comparison. Open source development will push into the mobile market just as it has in the server market, and we'll see devices like the Android/HTC G1 mobile take off and allow for a remarkable amount of flexibility in services. Libraries will be able to write software specifically for these devices rather than relying on second-layer information services like browsers to present their holdings. Imagine being able to write an application that would search your catalog and prompt the user to chat with a librarian if the search failed. Later in the book we will look at how this sort of application development is possible.

There is a popular law that governs the power and price of technology (specifically microchips, but it stands as a good predictive model for technology in general) called "Moore's law." Moore's law states that the number of transistors on a given chip will double every 18–24 months. This happens while price points for said chips remains reasonably stable. To translate into nonengineer speak, chips get twice as good just about every two years while remaining

the same price. This has been true since Gordon Moore first expli-
cated his law in 1958, over 50 years ago. For the mobile space, this
means that nonsmartphones will slowly be pushed out of the way
by more capable phones that cost the same amount to manufacture year after year. In five years, I don't believe there will be a
phone on the mainstream market that doesn't do what the average
smartphone does now. Libraries should get in front of this trend as
quickly as they can to ensure that we aren't playing catch-up the
way we have been with the social Web.

If librarians want to hold on to their roles as information selec-
tors and brokers, we need to be able to move toward reaching out
to our users through their preferred method of communication.
We've consistently moved into new communication methods, and
mobile isn't any different in that way. It's another avenue that our
patrons are using, and it's another way that we need to provide
information to them.

Mobile technology also has the ability to provide for services
and functions that have never existed before. One of the perceived
benefits in the advertising and marketing fields is that because the
cell phone is a personal device, as well as being location aware, it
acts as a far more efficient way to contact specific categories of users. For public libraries, for example, localization is a big deal, and
being able to focus their efforts on local users specifically, even
providing them with customized services on their cell phones, is a
huge opportunity.

Many libraries are already actively working to provide as many of
their services as possible to these new mobile patrons. Libraries as
varied as Yale Science Library (www.library.yale.edu/science/
textmsg.html), a public library consortia in Norway (http://
biblioteksvar.no/en/sms.html), and Southeastern Louisiana University (www.selu.edu/library/askref/text/index.html) are all using SMS messaging to provide basic reference service for their
patrons. In a later chapter, we will explore how you can provide
this service for your library as well, for no cost beyond some
personnel time to set it up.

As well, many libraries are providing specific interfaces for their
Web sites and catalogs that are mobile friendly. Some of these are
vendor specific, like the AirPAC from Innovative Interfaces, which

was a remarkably early model for mobile catalog access, hailing from way back in 2001. Lots of Innovative Interfaces libraries are still using AirPAC to provide services for their patrons, ranging from the King County Library System (http://catalog.kcls.org/airpac/search) to the Sunnyvale California Public Library (http://sunset.ci.sunnyvale.ca.us/airpac).

Other libraries, such as North Carolina State University (www.lib.ncsu.edu/m/), the University of Richmond (http://oncampus.richmond.edu/academics/libary/mobile/libmobilecat.htm), and Ball State University (www.bsu.edu/libraries/MOPAC/) are providing mobile catalog services in completely different ways. Further into the book, we'll examine how each of these schools is providing this service and outline ways that you can choose which method is right for you and your library.

These are just a few of the examples of the mobile technologies that you can learn to employ over the course of this book. We'll cover a host of other options, all with step-by-step instructions and best practices so that you can make the best decisions for your library and patrons.

▶ IMPORTANCE TO LIBRARIES

Libraries have always been places that people go to for information, but, with the explosion of mobile technology, our patrons are more and more expecting information to come to them rather than the other way around. People today are tied to the mobile phone as the center of their information ecosystem, and more and more these phones are providing an interface to nearly all of their informational needs.

In the same way that the personal computer spread from business to home use, the mobile phone has moved from Wall Street to become the fastest growing technology ever. The first commercially available mobile phone network was set up in Japan in 1979, and in less than 40 years worldwide penetration of mobile phones is over 50 percent, according to Reuters. More than half of the population of the planet have a mobile phone at this point, a rate of growth that exceeds the television, the VCR, and the personal computer. More people access the Internet via their cell phone than through a traditional PC when you look at statistics around the world. The importance of the mobile phone throughout the world as an information consumption device cannot be overstated, and if libraries ignore them as a platform, and as a general informational tool, it will prevent us from speaking the same language as our users.

In addition to preparing us for the expectations of our users, mobile phones are increasingly capable of providing services that have never been possible before. Most smartphones these days have GPS technology built in, as the cost of including it is negligible. With GPS, the phone becomes location aware, and the information it provides can reflect this. Location-specific information can be delivered for historical artifacts in a battlefield, for directional information in a city, or for relational information about the whereabouts of friends. The phone becomes a beacon, a transponder of more than just voice, and with this ability comes new and different ways that libraries can tap into their information stores and provide their patrons with information that even the patron didn't know they needed. In the Conclusion section of this book, I'll lay out some ways that I see location becoming important in the next five to ten years.

▶ PLATFORMS

The United States lags behind many countries throughout the world when it comes to its cellular infrastructure, largely because the densest metropolitan areas of the United States were some of the first in the world to have cellular coverage. In the 1980s, cellular service spread slowly through the larger U.S. cities, and then in the 1990s the rise of digital technologies led to further spreading across the country. Because of the need for backward compatibility, along with the financial strain on the providers, the spread of the second-generation and third-generation cellular technologies hasn't kept pace with that in some other parts of the world, where the initial buildup was less.

To understand the complexity of the mobile situation in the United States, this chapter will lay out the distinctions among carriers as well as among the leading operating systems that are driving the phones in question. The majority of this information won't directly affect the sorts of efforts that you may put forward in your library, but some of it may be important (for instance, when deciding what type of phone to buy for the best flexibility in moving from carrier to carrier).

The United States has four major cellular players nationally: AT&T, T-Mobile, Verizon, and Sprint. Each has different phones, and different carriers sometimes use completely different technologies with different capabilities. If you are deciding to purchase a mobile device for your library, the first question is probably just, "Which carrier has signal coverage in my library?" After determining this (and if you have more than one answer), there needs to be some way to determine how to make the decision. Sometimes that will be because of hardware. For example, AT&T is the only carrier in the United States that carries the iPhone, Verizon is the only carrier to have the BlackBerry Storm, and there are plenty of other exclusives from other carriers. You aren't tied to necessarily purchasing the hardware (the phone) from the provider, but most U.S. providers heavily subsidize the cost of the mobile phone if you purchase it with a contract for their service. This is roughly analogous to the razor-blade model of selling whereby you forego upfront profit (many phones are provided below cost, even free, with a contract) in order to reap the ongoing profit over time.

Technologically, the biggest difference between the various service providers is the type of radio used. AT&T and T-Mobile both use the GSM standard, while Verizon and Sprint use the CDMA standard. You don't need to know the technical differences between the ways that each works, but it may be important because phones sold in the United States will be for one or the other standard, but not both. If your library buys a phone based on capabilities, but doesn't pay attention to the systems it works with, you may find yourself with a surprise. On the other hand, the majority of people in the United States buy their device from the service provider directly, which nullifies the potential issues. This isn't the case necessarily in the rest of the world, where the market for "unlocked" phones that can be moved from provider to provider is larger.

Another factor that might impact your decision, especially if you will be traveling widely, is that the GSM standard is far more prevalent around the world than the CDMA. As a matter of fact, the United States is the only major market where CDMA is still widely deployed, so, if you are in a U.S. border state and expect to take the phone to Canada or Mexico, you might consider sticking with a GSM model.

The following sections provide a quick overview of each of the four major carriers and some minor players as well.

AT&T

Formerly known as Cingular, AT&T Mobility is the second largest mobile carrier in the United States. AT&T is notable for being the only carrier in the United States with the Apple iPhone. It maintains a 3G data network, but is sometimes criticized for coverage, especially in major cities. AT&T is a GSM network, the radio type that is most used around the globe.

> "3G" stands for 3rd Generation. The first 3G network was launched in Japan in 2001.

Verizon

The largest of the mobile carriers, Verizon has over 80 million subscribers in the United States. Notable hardware that is limited to Verizon includes the BlackBerry Storm (the only touch-screen–based BlackBerry). Verizon uses the CDMA network but is likely to be the first mobile provider to move to what's being called the Long Term Evolution (LTE) network. LTE is a fourth-generation cellular phone system that promises data speeds of at least 100 megabits per second.

Sprint

Third largest in terms of U.S. subscribers, Sprint made a splash in mid-2009 as the first carrier for the Palm Pre. Sprint is also a CDMA-based carrier.

T-Mobile

A distant fourth in terms of subscribers, T-Mobile stands out in most surveys of mobile users as having the best customer service of the big four. It also is a GSM-based network, like AT&T.

Minor Players

The smaller carriers in the United States, such as Tracfone and Virgin, are mostly prepaid cell providers. They sell you an inexpensive mobile phone, and you prepay for a set number of minutes. This is distinct from the more common contract-based approach of the big four, where you pay for a monthly allotment of minutes over the course of a one- or two-year contract. The prepay companies typically have no cellular infrastructure of their own. That is, they don't build towers and run lines; instead, they pay one of the main carriers to use their network, usually at a premium per-minute cost to the user.

The various network standards and radio types (CDMA for Sprint and Verizon, and GSM for AT&T and T-Mobile) mean that while you can, technically, buy a phone on the Sprint network (say, the new Palm Pre) and move it to the Verizon network (for the moment ignore the fact that phones are sometimes locked to specific carriers in software). You can't move an AT&T phone like the iPhone to the Verizon network, whether it is unlocked or not. The radio simply can't communicate with the towers across the two types. This bit of technical knowledge might come in handy, just to ensure that you aren't having expectations of the phones that aren't technically possible.

Phone Types

Most of the phones that we'll be looking at are known as smartphones. This isn't to say that other phones are dumbphones, just that there are commonalities between the so-called smartphones that set them apart from the majority of cell phones in the United States. In broad terms, the farther away from "phone" it gets, the smarter a smartphone becomes.

It is only during the past few years that mobile phone sales in the United States have begun swinging toward smartphones. The hallmarks of a smartphone as opposed to a non-smartphone are features like having a full QWERTY keyboard rather than just a numerical pad, a Web browser of some type, and some Personal Digital Assistant (PDA)–like functionalities (calendar, contacts, e-mail, etc.). Most smartphones require some form of data service in addition to the traditional phone minutes that are purchased with a cellular contract. At the same time, their functions go far beyond those of a "phone," really becoming pocket-sized computers capable of e-mail, messaging, editing documents, and more. In some cases, much, much, much more.

The following section will deal with the various types of handsets in broad overview, laying out just how varied the mobile space really is. It will also highlight the overall difficulties of developing a network based on specific carriers.

Windows Mobile

With Microsoft being the powerhouse that it is in the desktop computing space, one might expect it to have the leverage to ensure that any device that might need an operating system would be running a Microsoft OS. During the rise of the mobile phone, Microsoft attempted to find the right combination of features and speed that would allow its mobile operating system to become the de facto standard in the U.S. mobile market. It never quite got there, currently having just under 13 percent of the worldwide mobile smartphone market (as compared to around 90 percent of the desktop computer market). This hasn't stopped Microsoft from being very aggressive about ensuring that Windows Mobile is available on as many phones as possible.

Windows Mobile carries the overall aesthetic of the desktop versions of Windows over to the smartphone, with very similar behaviors and appearance. Users who are familiar with Windows XP should be capable of maneuvering the Windows Mobile interface well.

Developing a network for Windows Mobile is similar to developing one for the desktop version of Windows. The applications are built using standard Microsoft tools and languages, like Visual Studio and .NET. The difficulty comes in actually getting applications onto the devices. Until recently, there was no unified storefront to find and download applications from. Luckily for Windows Mobile users, Microsoft has launched the Windows Marketplace for Mobile. Modeled after the Apple iPhone App Store, it allows for direct-to-device downloads and management of its applications. To my knowledge, no libraries have developed applications specifically for the Windows Mobile platform.

iPhone and Apple SDK

In 2007, Apple released the iPhone, and in only two years it has become the smartphone that all other companies are chasing. While they took some time in allowing for the production of applications for the iPhone (it was over a year between the launch of the iPhone and the opening of the App Store), the model that Apple built in just 24 months is influencing the rest of the market to catch up.

Apple provided a public software development kit (SDK) at no cost, giving the public access to all of the tools needed to produce applications for the iPhone. The iPhone uses a version of the Apple Macintosh operating system, OS X, which makes the production of applications straightforward for anyone who has programmed for any Apple computer in the past three years or so. Apple does, however, control the distribution of applications by limiting the method by which you can load apps onto the iPhone. In order to get something onto the phone, whether a song, a movie, or an application, you have to go through iTunes. Via the iTunes store, Apple controls the applications that can run on the phone.

The development platform for the iPhone is similar to that for the Apple Macintosh, and it is based on Xcode. Anyone who is familiar with writing software for the current Apple operating system (OS X) should be able to pick up programming for the iPhone.

While the SDK is free, getting an application onto the iTunes Store isn't. In order to be hosted by Apple, a developer has to pay a $99.00 fee, and, if the application has a cost to the public, Apple asks for 30 percent of each sale. But a one-time $99.00 fee and no other charge if your application is free is quite a deal to get your library in front of the millions of iPhone users.

The barrier to entry is very low, and the upside could be enormous for a library in the right area. Hundreds of thousands of applications have been downloaded from the App Store, and libraries are just starting to explore the possibilities. The first application dedicated to a specific library was launched in January 2009 by the public library in Washington, DC, but over the course of 2009 I'm sure we'll see more of them.

Google and Android

In 2008, Google launched its first attempt at a mobile phone operating system, and it did so with a very interesting model. They open sourced the operating system, allowing any company that wished to manufacture the hardware, providing them with the underlying software free of charge. The first phone to take advantage of the new operating system, named Android, was brought to market by T-Mobile and is called the G1.

The biggest advantage of Android lies in its being open source, which means that developers can potentially add to the underlying operating system. Furthermore, having access to the operating system means that any applications developed for Android have the potential to tie more directly into the hardware of the phone in question and can tap into features like the accelerometer, digital compass, GPS, and camera. This level of access to the hardware is unheard of for developers on a mobile platform and may help to push the Android platform into a position of leadership among mobile devices.

Android may also become available on other, nonphone, hardware. Because it is an open platform, the possibility exists for it to be ported to any hardware, including netbooks and nonphone portable devices. If this happens (and it is very likely to), it will only help to push the Android market into more prominence, thus raising the attractiveness of the operating system in developers' eyes, which should result in more diverse and interesting applications.

Palm WebOS

Just as this book is being finished, Palm is releasing its brand new entry into the mobile phone market, an operating system called WebOS. The first device with WebOS is the Palm Pre. The Pre hasn't launched yet as this is being typed, but the early reviews put it as a solid contender to the iPhone for market share in the smartphone market.

Palm has announced that all applications for WebOS will be based on Web standards rather than on lower-level languages. This means that all of the applications for the Pre will be HTML/CSS/JavaScript and won't require more complex programming knowledge. This opens up the potential set of programmers for this platform to nearly anyone doing serious Web development.

> As the Pre and WebOS become more popular, check the wiki associated with this book for more news.

BlackBerry

The Canadian company Research in Motion's line of BlackBerry mobile phones is the undeniable leader in the U.S. market for business users. The success of the BlackBerry has been driven largely by business users who appreciate the instant "push" e-mail capabilities that exist between the mobile and a Blackberry e-mail server.

Development of the BlackBerry network revolves around the use of Java and the BlackBerry Java Development Environment (JDE). While very popular, it doesn't appear that any libraries have developed specifically for the BlackBerry set of phones.

Nokia

If you examined just the U.S. market for mobile phones, you would probably not guess that Nokia is the largest phone manufacturer in the world. The brand is underrepresented in the United States, given its share of the global market, with only a handful of phones offered by the mobile service providers. The most powerful of the modern Nokia phones in terms of processing and ability (the N95 and N97 models) have never been offered in the United States by a carrier.

Nokia phones use an operating system called Symbian, and the development software is, like BlackBerry's, a type of Java programming. Symbian relies primarily on the Java Micro Edition (JME), a version of the Java programming language that is written and optimized for mobile devices.

Netbooks

Netbooks are the largest growing segment of the nondesktop computer market, even though no one seems to be able to agree entirely on what distinguishes a netbook from a laptop. Very roughly, a netbook is a laptop that has a 12-inch or smaller screen, typically an Atom processor, and usually doesn't come with an internal CD/DVD ROM drive, instead relying on USB connectivity for anything beyond the internal drive. Depending on the manufacturer, the internal drive may also differ from that in the traditional laptop. Instead of being the traditional spinning-platter hard drive that relies on spinning magnetic discs and small, sensitive read/write heads in order to store and retrieve information, many netbooks use small solid-state hard drives (SSDs). SSDs have a much higher cost per megabyte but are far more durable, aren't sensitive to drops and shocks in the same way that a traditional hard drive is, and are more efficient in their energy consumption.

For the purposes of this book, netbooks are interesting because an increasing number of them are being sold with cellular radios built in, and they have the ability to maintain an Internet connection anywhere there is cellular signal. Many mobile companies are also beginning to treat netbooks like mobile phones in an economic sense, subsidizing them if customers agree to a data contract. While these are not expensive systems to begin with, typically costing between $250.00 and $400.00, with a cellular subsidy they are often simply given away for free (the company easily makes their money back over the cost of the contract).

Regardless of purchasing model, the netbook isn't a computer for everything. It is lower powered than most modern notebooks, but nearly all netbooks will easily handle the typical modern computing tasks: browsing the Web, playing video, word processing, and listening to audio. They may not be the best choice for higher-end computing tasks like editing video or 3D gaming, but for the price they deliver an impressive amount of power.

As with the smartphone, though, the power of ubiquitous connectivity is transformational. The netbook isn't as portable and accessible as the smartphone (while small, they aren't quite pocketable), but at the same time they don't suffer from some of the limitations. The resolution of the netbook screen is almost always near-standard and is never as limited in screen real estate as the smartphone. This means that netbooks, while an important mobile technology, don't require libraries to alter their current development or service models in the same kind of way as the expansion of the mobile phone, and the vast majority of this book will instead focus on the phone side of the mobile hardware divide.

Kindle and e-Books

Another hardware type that is also "always on" and connected via the cellular network are, increasingly, e-book readers. The most popular of the connected e-book readers is the Amazon Kindle, which is connected to the Sprint network. Unlike every other connected device that we've discussed here, the Kindle has a unique economic model. The device itself isn't subsidized, and Amazon covers the cost of the connectivity to the network in perpetuity for the life of the device. This means that while the cost of the Kindle is high, relative to other, nonconnected e-readers, you get Internet connectivity at no ongoing cost.

So what's the catch? Why isn't this the most popular connected device on the market? Because of the limitations of and the general technology that is used in the E Ink display.

E Ink is the name of the technology that drives these e-readers and is both their greatest advantage and greatest disadvantage. The advantage is that these displays are high contrast, allowing for a very paper-like reading experience, and consume remarkably little power. An E Ink display is, more or less, a layer of electrostatic spheres, where each sphere is half light and half dark. In order to create a "page," the spheres are flipped individually so that they make an image, and when the display needs to be changed, each sphere is flipped again to the new orientation. This provides an incredible resolution display, but it currently allows only for mono-chrome (at the current high end, a 16-level grayscale is the best available) and is very slow to refresh.

For most of the modern Web, this is a difficult proposition to deal with. The browser on the Kindle can't handle lots of the parts of the Web (no Flash support, no video at all, nothing dynamic), and thus the best that you can expect from the Kindle browser is a text-based page. It might work for some emergency e-mail check-ing, or for reading static pages, but, compared to even the most ru-dimentary browser on a smartphone, the experience leaves much to be desired. Still, there is something to say for no-contract, al-ways-on, ubiquitous connectivity, as simple as it may be. It is de-signed, after all, to act as just enough connectivity to allow you to purchase books on the go from the Amazon store. At that, it works beautifully—you can get any of tens of thousands of books deliv-ered wirelessly in about a minute to your device, anywhere that you have cellular signal.

At the time of this writing, two other e-book readers have been announced that include cellular connectivity, the Sony Reader Daily Edition and the Plastic Logic Reader. Both connect to 3G networks, and both of the companies brokered a deal with AT&T to provide cellular connectivity. However, unlike the Amazon Kin-dle, which has at least a rudimentary Web browser, neither the Sony nor the Plastic Logic 3G-capable e-readers appear to have a browser as a part of their software. Early reports are that both lack any connectivity past online purchasing of content.

One piece of huge news for libraries that has just come to light is that Sony has partnered with Overdrive to allow owners of the Sony Reader Daily Edition, at least, and possibly other versions of the Sony Reader, to check out books to the reader via the Over-drive service at their local library. Details on how this will work, lim-itations, and other details haven't been released yet.

Look for more information on this through the updated links via Delicious, details of which are provided in the book's Conclu-sion.

Other Devices

Within just the past few years, mobile carriers have begun brokering deals with nonphone hardware makers to include cellular connectivity inside other types of devices. Most notably, the rise of the netbook class of laptop computer and the growth of electronic readers (e-readers) have pushed the always-on mobile Internet options into nonphone spaces. While neither of these (netbooks, e-readers) has the same communication profile as a phone (can't call from either, no SMS directly), they each have their own limitations and potential for use in libraries.

When deciding where to throw your development time and energy, keep in mind not only the overall statistics (BlackBerry has the largest installed base of smartphones in the United States, and Nokia is the largest seller of mobile phones in the world) but also local trends. Pay attention to the sorts of phones you see in your library. Look at your Web site logs and see what sorts of mobile browsers are visiting. And, if developing a native application seems out of the question, whether due to time, talent, or other reasons, you can always concentrate on Web development. Provide a mobile Web site instead of a native app, and you lose some abilities, but you still provide a lot of functionality to your patrons.

▶2

PLANNING

▶ Become Part of Your Patrons' Information Ecosystem

▶ Get Staff Buy-In

▶ Explore the Uses of Mobile Technologies

▶ Develop/Customize Mobile Apps for Your Library

▶ Provide Mobile Database Access

▶ BECOME PART OF YOUR PATRONS' INFORMATION ECOSYSTEM

Like all library services, how to move into the mobile space depends on the needs of your patrons. There are certainly lots of cost/benefit analyses to do before launching any new service in libraries, but there are several good reasons to move forward with mobile services. Although some have already been mentioned, they bear repeating because of their centrality to the issue of mobile services.

Moving forward with mobile services means that you are, even more than with other forms of virtual reference, becoming a part of your patrons' information ecosystem. When patrons can access the information they need at a moment's notice, wherever they happen to be, the library becomes something portable. Instead of insisting that your patrons be somewhere specific (at your reference desk, in front of a computer, on campus), you are allowing them to be anywhere and doing anything and still touch the library. It's a very powerful interaction, and, depending on the types of mobile services you offer, you extend portions of your services and collections beyond your walls and out to wherever your patrons are.

As an example of this extension, consider just your reference service. At a point not that long in the past, in order for a patron to interact with and request information from a librarian, the patron had to come into the library itself. All service was synchronous, face-to-face service. The introduction of the telephone shortened the distance that people had to go in order to get library assistance, but it didn't revolutionize the service to the point where a new model was necessary. In most libraries, except perhaps the very largest public libraries, telephone and face- to-face reference coexisted happily. The introduction of e-mail and instant messaging (IM) over the past 20 years has caused some model changes to occur, mainly because of the ability of both e-mail and IM to queue asynchronously. A backup of these services can occur quickly, and in some ways the virtuality of these communications makes it more difficult to handle than face-to-face backup.

Adding mobile reference to the mix does change things. Mobile reference means that your patrons can contact you anywhere they are; it puts a direct line to your reference staff literally in their pocket. While it's true that they could call you, more and more often the current generation defaults to texting and SMS (Short Message Service) for communications, and adding them as options for them to contact you, while powerful, is something to plan carefully for.

Some risk is associated with any extension of services. In some situations you can absolutely be a victim of your own success and position your library for more than it can handle. While, as they say, it is the right problem to have, it is still a problem. Moving your library into the mobile sphere with services is one area where demand could very quickly outstrip supply. This isn't to say that your library should hesitate in offering said services (and we'll see why in the next section), but to suggest adding caution and awareness to any rollout.

Managing expectations is a large part of any service offering. If you manage your customer's expectations, you are halfway to a positive interaction before you even start. When attempting to manage mobile expectations, most of the effort will have to be put into the manner in which the service is advertised, but setting service guidelines for staff who aren't familiar with the expectations of this type of interaction is another area worth spending some training on. Not everyone may be familiar with the norms of texting, as just one example of mobile communication.

As phones become more and more powerful, the expectations of our users are changing as well. Libraries are well acquainted with the change in generational expectations for information. We've spent years moving from print to electronic for collections, catalogs, and services. As every new generation of the twentieth century matured, they brought with them specific expectations about how they gather and interact with information and, thus, libraries. New services like Twitter, Facebook, and FriendFeed are changing the way that people communicate online, and new tools like Evernote and Google Docs are changing the way that people interact with their own information. Communication and personal information are increasingly moving into what is commonly called "the cloud," which is shorthand for server-based, synchronized information on all of your devices at once. Cloud-based information is information that is available wherever you are, whatever you are using. The next generation of patrons is going to expect the same integration and ubiquity in services that they now are starting to expect in storage.

So, think of all of the things your library does, from acquisitions to instruction. How can these things be embedded in people's lives? What could you accomplish if your patrons could be in contact with you not at *any* point in their day, but at *every* point in their day?

▶ GET STAFF BUY-IN

Any change in a library brings with it both opportunity and outcry—often both, and from both patrons and staff! There are so many pieces to the mobile library experience that diving in and doing even a significant portion of them would be a huge undertaking for even the largest and best-staffed and best-funded libraries. Choose your first steps toward mobilization carefully is the best advice. That, and careful planning, will get you through the stages of change.

Considering that librarians are notoriously change averse, I suggest that the best way to think about getting buy-in for making services more mobile friendly is to consider the five stages of grief, originally laid out by Elisabeth Kübler-Ross in her 1969 book *On Death and Dying*. Those are, in order: Denial, Anger, Bargaining, Depression, and Acceptance. Getting buy-in from people excited about a change isn't hard. The hard part is getting buy-in from people who aren't excited, or are even hostile, to the change. Thus, the Five Stages of Grief is a change model you can use.

Denial

One of the first steps in any project is justifying it. The most common objection to any project is "why do we need to be doing that?", which is just another way of saying "we don't need to be doing that." Denial of the need for these new services is more difficult to overcome in certain areas than in others. An academic library is going to have a hard time denying that college students want mobile services, and, if asked, college students will presumably say that they are very interested in them. In a public library setting, however, this might not be so straightforward, especially depending on the demographic of your particular population. The rest of the book you are currently holding will hopefully provide enough statistics and other proof that mobile devices are growing at a rate that can't be ignored.

Anger

Hopefully the shortest of the stages in a professional change, anger can be associated with any significant alteration in duties or responsibilities in the workplace. In the case of the move toward mobile services, anger could be focused at the patron ("I'm angry because what they want is stupid") or at the change agent in the library in question ("I'm angry because so-and-so is making my job harder"). Getting past this stage requires time to show how mobile technology increases the flexibility of the library staff, allowing them to be more effective in their jobs. Focusing on the increased capability on the part of the staff and not on the potential burden helps overcome the potential for anger.

Bargaining

This stage is all about continuing to justify the old way of doing things and is a passive-aggressive way of being change averse. The bargaining staff member will find reasons that the old way was better or that the library can still reach out but maybe one particular piece of the mobile service isn't needed. To deal confidently with the Bargainer means having done a good job of transparently planning the new services and having the staff be a part of the implementation. If you have everyone on board prior to the roll out, you can keep this stage to a bare minimum.

Depression

This stage is a combination of the sadness of something being lost (our once-comfortable isolation from the every whim of our patrons) and the intrinsic discomfort that happens during a shift in workplace responsibilities. Depression is another stage that hopefully is short-lived, and staff should move through it as they become familiar with the new services and comfortable with communicating with patrons via mobile channels.

Acceptance

The last stage is acceptance, where everyone realizes the inevitability of the move to mobile technologies. Preferably, staff should more than "accept" the new service models and informational structures. They should embrace and enhance them. This may take some time to happen, especially for the non-change-agents. But acceptance in the face of the overwhelming evidence of need for these services should happen relatively quickly, especially in terms of library change.

Some libraries have already passed through these stages and have gotten themselves into the business of mobile in various ways. The next section will discuss the current activities that libraries are doing in the mobile space, from mobile reference to providing content to your patron's cell phone. While I think the real flowering of the mobile space is probably a year or two away, some libraries are trying and succeeding with mobile now. For those that aren't, take a look at what is being done, and see where you might be able to jump in.

▶ EXPLORE THE USES OF MOBILE TECHNOLOGIES

We've been discussing mobile technologies as something future oriented, but lots of libraries are already exploring the various ways of utilizing mobile technologies to help patrons. Here are just a few features that libraries have become involved in.

SMS

Many libraries use SMS as a part of their reference service (see list at http://libsuccess.org/index.php?title=Online_Reference# Libraries_Offering_SMS_Reference_Services). Some use a dedicated commercial SMS service like those offered by Altarama and Upside Wireless or by actually purchasing a dedicated cellular phone for reference use. Others use a very popular hack that allows SMS messages to be done with AOL Instant Messenger (AIM). In the case of the AIM interface, you can leverage SMS reference into your existing IM or chat reference service, usually with very little difficulty.

In addition to using SMS for reference services, many libraries have instituted SMS notifications regarding materials. Notification that a request has been filled, reminders of when materials are due, and other library system–related communications can be sent via SMS. This is usually a one-way communication, going out to the patron, rather than the two-way communication of the reference interview. But broadcasting information in this manner can be powerful, especially if you put together an opt-in system for announcements or other library updates.

Web Site Mobility

Ensuring that your Web site is appropriately designed for mobile browsers is becoming easier and easier, because mobile browsers are becoming better and better. Just a few years ago, you would have needed to code two different versions of your site if you wanted it to appear properly on both the desktop and on phones. Now, with better use of Web standards and the availability of conditional CSS (cascading style sheet), you can get a very functional mobile version of your site with just a little tweaking.

Many of the libraries that are using both mobile OPACs and mobile Web sites can be found at the Library Success Wiki at http://libsuccess.org/index.php?title=M-Libraries#Mobile_interfaces. These libraries have adopted commercial products like the AirPAC from Innovative Interfaces and library-coded OPAC interfaces and have created general mobile-specific Web sites.

Mobile Reference

Some libraries use mobile phones as a sort of on-the-go reference device, being able to surf the Web, look up quick reference questions, search the catalog, and more, all from a single portable device. Having a device like the iPhone or the G1 with you while doing roaming reference effectively puts the phone, IM, and Web browser with you all the time.

Bluetooth

Most modern phones use a wireless communications standard called Bluetooth to communicate information over short distances. Bluetooth is the protocol that is used by the wireless headsets you see sticking out of ears all over these days. But while here in the United States it is only being used for wireless microphones and car buds, across the world Bluetooth is used for a huge number of things. For example, it can be used to transfer files onto a mobile phone, turning it into a wireless thumb drive.

Of course, any phone with Bluetooth has the capability of receiving files as well. This is something that the technology wizards at the Delft Library Concept Center in the Netherlands, more popularly known as DOK (http://dok.info/index.php?cat=pagina& pagina_id=110) have exploited. They have Bluetooth stations where you can "check out" media directly to your cell over Bluetooth, and when you enter the library they push welcome text to your mobile as well.

▶ DEVELOP/CUSTOMIZE MOBILE APPS FOR YOUR LIBRARY

The first consolidated storefront for a mobile phone platform for applications was the Apple iPhone App Store, which opened on July 10, 2008. The iPhone App Store wasn't the first place that applications were available for mobile phones, as independent developers could write for a number of mobile platforms prior to the App Store. However, it was the first to be a vertically integrated store; unless you hack your phone, the App Store is the only place you can get applications for your iPhone. The applications are purchased, downloaded, and managed by the same software, iTunes, which manages the other aspects of the iPhone ecosystem, like music, movies, syncing of information, and backup. But before the App Store, there were still places to get applications for your devices.

One of the very earliest examples of a mobile device with robust application development was the Palm OS devices. From the very early days of the Palm Pilot, there were third-party applications being written and sold for the Palm. These added abilities that the device itself didn't come with, like the ability to read e-books or to edit Microsoft Word files. In the end, the reason that applications for mobile devices are popular is that no device maker can include every possible need—not every person has identical needs in a mobile device. Applications allow users to customize the functions of their mobile phones and to extend their existing functions. Modern mobile phones are effectively small computers, and the expectation is that you will be able to install programs much like you do with your personal computer.

Some libraries are experimenting with developing and providing their own apps for the iPhone. The first library-specific application for the iPhone was put out by the District of Columbia

Public Library (DCPL) under the direction of Aaron Schmidt. It allows users to search the catalog, identifies which branch of the library has the item, and allows users to put a hold on an item and choose a pickup location. It also has the hours for all the branches, addresses of the branches that link to Google Maps on the phone, and a phone number that dials with a single click.

The DCPL has released the code for their app under a Creative Commons Attribution-Noncommercial-Share Alike 3.0 United States License. The code is available on their Web site (http://dclibrarylabs.org/dcpl-iphone-app-code-available) for other libraries to study and adapt, so hopefully others will begin to extend the capabilities of this application. To develop an application for the iPhone, you must sign up as an Apple Developer at the Apple Web site (http://developer.apple.com/iphone/program). The Software Development Kit for the iPhone is free, but in order to actually publish an application in the App Store, you have to sign up with Apple at a cost of $99.00. Development for the iPhone is very much like development for OS X on a Macintosh computer, and if you have a programmer who has done any of the latter, the former should come pretty easily.

Another entry into the App Store of interest to libraries is the OCLC WorldCat application. It is designed to use the iPhone GPS to find the closest OCLC member library with a given book or to simply locate and map the library for the user. Between this, and the blossoming of individual library Apps, there are lots of possibilities for the future of library applications on mobile phones.

The iPhone App Store has been successful beyond most expectations. In less than a year, there have been thousands of applications written for the iPhone and hundreds of millions of downloads of these applications. Apple reported in March 2009 that there were more than 25,000 applications available and that more than 800 million downloads had occurred from the App Store. No other mobile device has even approached this level of customization and application availability. It has been so successful that every other major phone operating system is in the process of rolling out their own application store to be built in to their handsets. Windows Mobile is launching an integrated store named SkyMarket, Google has Market in place now for its Android handsets, Research in Motion is preparing its BlackBerry App World, and even Nokia is preparing a mobile application store called "Ovi." All are hoping to replicate the success of the Apple model, integrating the third-party software into their hardware and being gatekeepers for the sorts of software allowed on their devices.

The Google Android operating system has the Android Market, which is similar to the App Store in function, although the programming environment is very different. Google provides a Software Development Kit (SDK) for Android, and because the operating system itself is open source, there is a much higher level of understanding of what's happening at the operating system level. There is a lot of possibility in development for Android devices. The primary language for Android development is Java, and the fact that there isn't currently any library-specific applications for the G1 has more to do with its time-in-market and overall popularity than the lack of need.

Unfortunately, all of the stores (except the Apple and the Android) won't be up and running prior to press time for this book. But the iPhone App Store points the way toward some of the possibilities for these applications for library use, and the Google Android Market has a few tricks up its sleeve as well.

For libraries, the most interesting applications in either app store are the electronic book (e-book) readers. There are many applications, but the three that I will discuss are outstanding for the iPhone and iPod Touch: Stanza, Amazon Kindle, and Classics. I will also briefly discuss one of the mobile Web sites worth visiting: Google Books Mobile.

Stanza

Stanza is an application that allows for nearly anything you might want to do with an e-book (see Figure 2.1). It gives you instant access to Project Gutenberg, the home of more than 25,000 public domain books, free for download. It also has access to a number of other e-bookstores, from the general purpose (Fictionwise) to the specialized (O'Reilly or All Romance). The latter ones sell e-books, ranging in price from a couple of dollars to $12.00 or more. Stanza also has a desktop application for your computer that will allow you to convert and upload existing texts,

▶ Figure 2.1: Stanza Main Screen

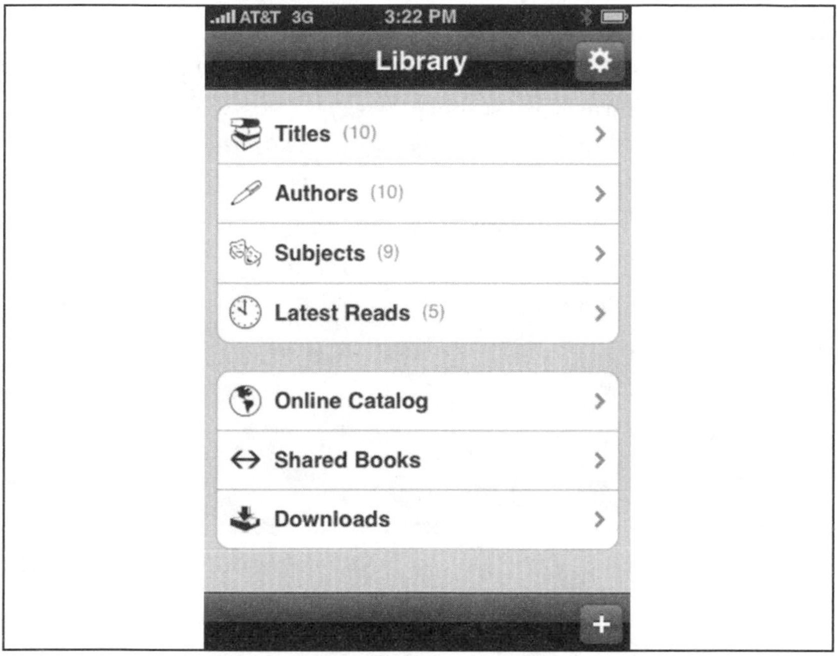

from Word files to converted PDFs, to your phone. The interface is well done and allows you to customize the text display and alter the colors, sizes, spacing, and other features in order to make reading from the screen as comfortable as possible. You can also bookmark positions in the books, to return to at any point. The flexibility of this application, and the access to the thousands and thousands of texts in Project Gutenberg and Feedbooks (another source of public domain titles), make it an absolute must-have download for the iPhone. The best part is that it's free.

Kindle

The Amazon Kindle application is the companion application to the hardware e-book reader produced by Amazon. It allows you to purchase books at Amazon and have them delivered wirelessly to your iPhone or iPod Touch. You can't yet purchase books directly from the application, but this seems such an obvious upgrade that I can only imagine it will be added as a feature soon. Buying a book at Amazon works seamlessly with Kindle, though, and the Amazon Store really is the enormous advantage that Amazon has over all of the other e-book applications (see Figures 2.2 and 2.3). As of this writing, the Amazon Kindle store contains over 260,000 books. It is by a wide margin the largest e-bookstore in the world. One of the features of the mobile application that is useful for individuals, but not likely to be useful to libraries, is called Whispersync. If you have multiple Kindles attached to your account, whether the actual Kindle e-book reader or the application on the iPhone, you can go back and forth between them, and Whispersync will keep your place for you, syncing your furthest read location from one to the other as needed.

Classics

The App simply called Classics (see Figure 2.4) is somewhat odd compared to the other two e-book apps. It doesn't have a store. In-

▶ Figure 2.2: Kindle Launch Screen

▶ Figure 2.3: Kindle Main Screen

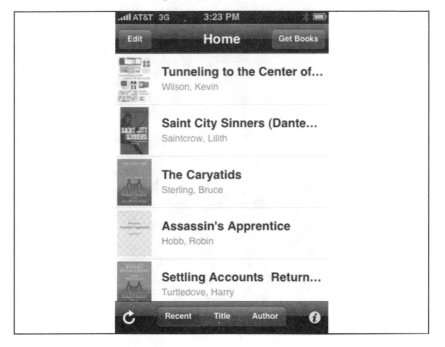

stead, it comes loaded with around 20 public domain works. It is also the only paid app in this group, even if it is only 99 cents. But what you get for your dollar is a thing of beauty, really an outstanding-looking application. Compare its screenshot in Figure 2.4 with those of Stanza and Kindle in Figures 2.1 and 2.3, and you can see the difference that presentation makes. Not only does the launch screen look amazing, but the pages even render with a touch-sensitive page turn effect. If the specific works in Classics (currently books such as *Alice in Wonderland, Pride and Prejudice,* and *Frankenstein*) answer a collection development need for you, it is a phenomenal value for the readability and ease of use of the application.

Google Books Mobile

One more e-book reading option should be mentioned: the Google Books Mobile project (see Figure 2.5). Google has formatted almost 2.5 million books, all of which are in the public domain,

▶ Figure 2.4: Classics Main Screen

▶ Figure 2.5: Google Books

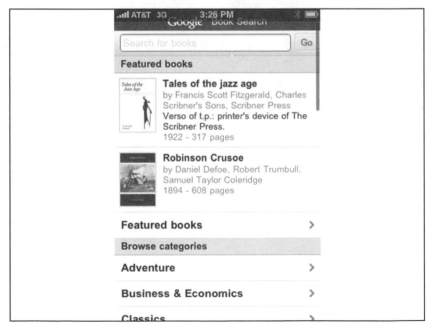

from their library scanning project for use on mobile phones. Using the Web browser on nearly any smartphone, you can search and read any of these books, making Google Books the largest e-book library in the world. And accessing them doesn't involve any particular software or any particular phone or operating system.

At the time of this writing, there is only one mobile-specific application for libraries, the District of Columbia Public Library application written for the Apple iPhone. As well, the Google Android platform is beginning to gather support, and both Black-Berry and Windows Mobile have announced that they will have applications stores open this year. Expect to see quite a few library applications pop up on mobile devices over the next two to three years.

▶ PROVIDE MOBILE DATABASE ACCESS

Your library, more than likely, provides some database access to its patrons. You almost certainly don't have the ability to alter the look and feel of the database for mobile users, though. Recognizing this, some database vendors are providing mobile-specific interfaces for their products. The list is still reasonably small compared to the number of database vendors libraries deal with, but we should expect that this trend will continue to move through other vendors. If you have a specific database that your patrons rely on, and they want a mobile version, tell your vendor about it.

Factiva
http://mobile.beta.factiva.com

Factiva is one of the most important business databases in the world, so it's no surprise that Factiva joined the mobile ranks quickly. The introduction page to Factiva Mobile says that it provides:

▶ Snapshots of key information for over two million private and public companies worldwide

> ▶ Continuous news updates about the companies relevant to you
> ▶ Current stock quotes
> ▶ The latest executive information

Unsurprisingly, Factiva seems to be designed specifically for BlackBerry devices, which makes sense as BlackBerry is by far the market leader in smartphones for business use.

Westlaw
http://west.thomson.com/software/wireless/default.aspx

Westlaw has a useful mobile Web site, but the appearance given after looking at their descriptions of their mobile access is that they haven't updated them in some time. They have software available for the Palm OS but not for the three market leaders in smartphones. Some of the hardware they reference is a decade old. With that said, the mobile site is clean and works well on most mobile browsers.

PubMed
http://pubmedhh.nlm.nih.gov/nlm/pubmed/index.html

PubMed's mobile site allows you to do both a basic search and a limited amount of specialized searching, like Systematic Reviews and Clinical Queries. One disadvantage is that if you browse on to an actual article, you get forwarded to the regular, nonmobile, target site. This may be the case with the other mobile sites listed here, but as you have to have a login for them, I was unable to test actual article retrieval.

Hoover's
www.hooversmobile.com

Hoover's appears to have the most current of all the mobile database sites that I visited. They have an admittedly interesting way of limiting access to their iPhone-specific Web site (you must register, and they text you the link to the site). But the site itself is optimized for the iPhone very well and looks great. They also have applications for BlackBerry and Windows Mobile, the latter of which is a paid service.

Who will be affected (e.g., reference, IT, circulation) and how will the various parts of the library work together to provide these new services? The implementation of a new service should always be examined holistically in a library. Any new service has the possibility of affecting disparate parts of the library, but mobile services might be more insidious than some. Services that are offered help to set patron expectations for the rest of their interactions with the library, and it is to the benefit of the library as a whole to be fully on board with mobile applications as you move forward.

With that said, mobile services are typically focused around one or two departments, and can be introduced department by department until the entire library is comfortable with them. If implementing SMS reference, it is obviously the reference department that is going to end up being the leader in implementation. Planning involves the same sort of issues that you have with any new program. You will need to set expectations for response to need (how long will a mobile user wait for a reply?), and with reference there is always the discussion about priorities of interaction (if you have multiple contacts simultaneously, how do you prioritize?).

▶3

IMPLEMENTATION

- ▶ Create a Mobile Library Web Site
- ▶ Make Your OPAC Mobile
- ▶ Create Portable Instructional Resources
- ▶ Offer Mobile Library Tours
- ▶ Offer Mobile Collections
- ▶ Provide SMS Services in Your Library
- ▶ Explore Other Implementation Ideas

After a lot of discussion earlier in this book about why mobile technology is so important, this chapter is designed to let you get your feet wet in providing mobile services. It will walk through a variety of different ways of moving into mobile and through the process of developing these various services. Each section should stand alone, so, if you aren't interested in coding, you can safely skip those sections without fear of missing something. But if you want to learn to code CSS for a mobile site, I'm hoping that there's enough meat in this section to get you through the basics.

At the same time, don't be afraid of taking a look at the code, even if you aren't a coder. I'll explain what the code is doing as I go, and, honestly, it doesn't take much code these days to accomplish some really great results.

▶ CREATE A MOBILE LIBRARY WEB SITE

Chances are, your library has a Web site. Whether that Web site is a relatively simple one that lists your hours and some basic information or is a full-fledged virtual branch with interactivity and a multiplicity of services, both are valuable. And neither is as valuable as it could be if it doesn't render well on mobile devices. Most libraries want to be as available as possible to their patrons, and making your Web site friendly to mobile browsers can be an incredibly powerful way of connecting directly to them. And, with just a little planning, it doesn't have to be a struggle.

Web Standards

The most important way to ensure that your Web site will look good on a tiny screen and on who knows what browser is to stick to standard Web coding. The standards for Web development are wide ranging, but there are a few basics. The group that recommends standards for the Web is known as the World Wide Web Consortium (W3C). As the W3C says on its About page (www .w3.org/Consortium):

> W3C primarily pursues its mission through the creation of Web standards and guidelines. Since 1994, W3C has published more than 110 such standards, called W3C Recommendations. W3C also engages in education and outreach, develops software, and serves as an open forum for discussion about the Web. In order for the Web to reach its full potential, the most fundamental Web technologies must be compatible with one another and allow any hardware and software used to access the Web to work together. W3C refers to this goal as "Web interoperability." By publishing open (non-proprietary) standards for Web languages and protocols, W3C seeks to avoid market fragmentation and thus Web fragmentation.

Content versus Style

In addition to a discussion of the actual coding standards, it isn't out of place to remind anyone designing a Web site these days that the separation of content and style is absolutely necessary for Web pages. If you started coding Web sites very early in the days of the

Web, you learned to put style information (fonts, colors, positions, etc.) into the actual HTML document, like this:

```
<font size="4" color="red">This text is red and
    size 4</font>
<font size="3" color="blue">This text is blue
    and size 3</font>
<font face="verdana" color="green">Here is a
    section with a different font and color</font>
```

Positioning was usually done with the use of tables and, believe it or not, invisible GIF files of specific sizes used to push objects where you needed them.

This worked fine in the very early days of the Web, but it becomes inflexible and inelegant when dealing with large numbers of Web pages or when you want really fine control over positioning and text. The current Web standard is to separate content from style in the form of HTML and CSS (cascading style sheet). The HTML (or, in some cases, XHTML), is the content part, where you just have the raw information, with no colors, positions, or other style elements. The CSS file controls the style, telling the browser how the content of the HTML should look. Because of this separation, you can tell a given type of browser to display different things, to position things differently, and to give each browser type the best-looking layout possible.

Warning: Mild tech talk ahead.

There are multiple ways of directing patrons to your mobile site, but the easiest is to write specific CSS for your mobile site and then have that CSS served from a specific URL just for mobile users. Most sites seem to use some variation of either subdomain or directory-specific address. For example:

If your main URL is: http://www.library.edu
Then your mobile site would be either: http://m.library.edu *or* http://www.library.edu/m

These would serve your mobile style sheet, while the standard URL continues to serve the full browser experience. This allows patrons to access the mobile-specific site while leaving your main Web site untouched.

This isn't the best method, though, because it requires that your patrons know that you have a mobile site in advance of visiting. Best-case scenario in this situation is that you have a "mobile users click here" link to forward them to the mobile version, which is still a subpar experience for a user.

Using a Mobile CSS

A better method uses conditional CSS. This is simply a statement that gives a parameter for when to use a specific CSS file instead of your regular CSS. It is an "if" statement, in logical terms. One example of such a statement would be:

```
<link media="only screen and (max-device-width:
    480px)" href="mobile.css" type="text/css"
    rel="stylesheet" />
```

This code in your HTML file tells the browser, in effect, that if the device that is calling this particular Web page has a maximum screen resolution of 480 pixels (the resolution of the iPhone and iPod Touch screens) then it should use the mobile.css style to display. Because of the max-device-width command, phones with lower resolution screens (almost every smartphone on the market) will also get caught by this statement. Anything with a larger screen resolution, like any browser running on a desktop or laptop system, will display the normal CSS file for the page.

With that little tiny bit of code, you can make nearly any page into an attractive mobile version by causing the page to call a mobile.css file when it sees a specific screen size device trying to access it. The mobile.css file can then reshape the page to the appropriate dimensions, eliminate visual clutter, and generally streamline the interface for the patron. It also doesn't require your patron to know anything about your site before visiting, use different addresses, or anything else. It just works.

Like anything you program, there are literally an infinite number of ways to achieve the end. Any language that is parsed by a browser could be used to generate the if–then statement and shift the rendering from normal to mobile.css. That is, as long as the browser in question doesn't have that particular language disabled. There are a number of mobile browsers that aren't as capable as standard ones and may not deal with JavaScript properly. You should think about this possibility when deciding how to mobilize your site.

With the little bit of HTML code given earlier, you can cause a page to call a mobile.css file when it sees a specific screen size device trying to access it. But what would that CSS look like? For the purposes of a mobile site, you want to focus on getting the width right as well as stripping out images and focusing on the navigation.

Because the possible number of mobile browsers and devices is so high, to develop for only one resolution, while easier, isn't the best option. There are lots of sites that are developing "iPhone-specific" styles, because the vast majority of mobile browsing these days is done with the iPhone (http://marketshare.hitslink.com/report.aspx?qprid=10). But to ignore the other possibilities when you can include them seems irresponsible.

The CSS for the width of a mobile site needs to be able to be viewed appropriately at any resolution between about 100 pixels and 480 pixels. For this, you really do need to focus on just a list of links or on a very tight, relatively spaced set of images. For the purposes of discussion, let's take a look at one library in particular: the Skokie Public Library in Skokie, Illinois. Their nonmobile Web site looks like Figure 3.1—very visual, colorful, and a lot of things going on. There's a full left-hand navigation menu, along with some top image navigation, images on the right for decoration, and just generally lots of choices for the patron.

A sample of the CSS code for the page shown in Figure 3.1 would look like this:

```
/* CSS Document */
/*
Base Colors
#19314B - Body background
#701F99 - Reading
#D12D33 - Movies
#F8A91C - Research
```

▶ Figure 3.1: Skokie Public Library Web Site (http://skokielibrary.info)

```
#1F73B2 - Events
#608E3A - Teens
#EF6F19 - Kids
*/
body {
background-color : #19314B;
font-size: small;
margin: 0px;
margin-left: 0px;
margin-right: 0px;
margin-top: 0px;
margin-bottom: 0px;
color: #333333;
}
div, p, td, th, blockquote, li {
font-family : arial, helvetica, sans-serif;
font-size: small;
color : #333333;
}
form {
font-family : arial, helvetica, sans-serif;
font-size: small;
color : #333333;
}
```

```
input, textarea, checkbox, radio, select, option
   {
font-family : arial, helvetica, sans-serif;
font-size: small;
color : #333333;
background-color: #FFFFFF;
}
p {
margin-top: .5em;
padding-bottom: 0px;
padding-top: 0px;
margin-bottom: .5em;
}
ul {
padding-top: 0px;
padding-bottom: 0px;
margin-top: 0px;
margin-bottom: 0px;
}
ol {
padding-top: 0px;
padding-bottom: 0px;
margin-top: 0px;
margin-bottom: 0px;
}
div.feature p {
margin-top: .25em;
padding-bottom: 0px;
padding-top: 0px;
margin-bottom: .3em;
}
div.feature h3 {
margin-top: 1em;
}
div.top_highlight p {
margin-top: .25em;
padding-bottom: 0px;
padding-top: 0px;
margin-bottom: .3em;
}
div.top_highlight h3 {
margin-top: 1em;
```

```
}
a:link, a:visited, a:active {
color: #330099;
/* font-family: Arial, Helvetica, sans-serif; */
text-decoration: underline;
}
a:hover {
color: #330099;
/* font-family: Arial, Helvetica, sans-serif; */
text-decoration: underline;
}
```

. . . and on and on . . . for over 1,183 lines! It's a really complex CSS file, with a ton of specialized styles for features like JavaScript slideshows and more. But it takes into account all of the style information for their entire site.

Now take a look at their mobile site in Figure 3.2. See the difference? The mobile site is just about as bare bones as you can get, with nothing more than text links and a logo. The impressive part is the way that they've distilled their entire site down to just the in-

▶ Figure 3.2: Skokie Public Library Mobile Web Site (http://m.skokielibrary.info)

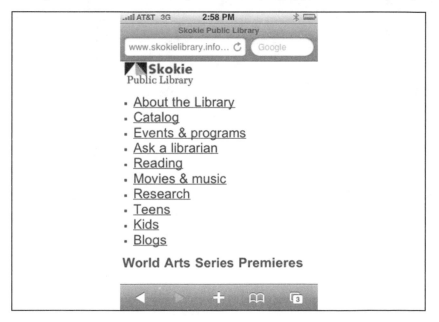

formation that you need, without any of the visual overhead. My favorite aspect of this site, and one of the most clever, is the way they integrated their blogs by repurposing the RSS feeds into the mobile version. Very clever, and nicely done! Also worth noting is the way that they integrated news and events into the site, with easy-to-read updates about what's going on in the near future at the library.

For parity, here's the mobile CSS:

```css
/* CSS Document */
body {
background-color : #FFFFFF;
font-size: small;
margin: 0px;
margin-left: 4px;
margin-right: 0px;
margin-top: 0px;
margin-bottom: 0px;
color: #333333;
}
div, p, td, th, blockquote, li, em, strong, h1,
   h2, h3, h4 {
font-family: arial, helvetica, sans-serif;
font-size: small;
color : #333333;
}
/* li { margin-left: -50px; } */
h1, h2, h3, h4 {
font-weight: bold;
}
form {
font-family : arial, helvetica, sans-serif;
font-size: small;
color : #333333;
}
input, textarea, checkbox, radio, select, option
   {
font-family : arial, helvetica, sans-serif;
font-size: small;
color : #333333;
background-color: #FFFFFF;
```

```
}
p {
margin-top: .5em;
padding-bottom: 0px;
padding-top: 0px;
margin-bottom: .5em;
}
ul {
margin-left:2px;
padding-left:16px;
list-style-type:square;
}
ol {
margin-left:20px;
padding-left:16px;
padding-top: 0px;
padding-bottom: 0px;
margin-top: 0px;
margin-bottom: 0px;
}
div.feature img {
display: none;
}
blockquote {
text-indent: 0px;
margin-left: 0px;
}
.little_text {
font-size: x-small;
}
div.hp_bottom {
display: none;
}
```

That's it! That's the whole mobile CSS file: 66 lines, or just about 5 percent of the total size of the full site. This speaks to the degree to which you must pare down and simplify your site when you move to mobile. Even if you don't speak CSS, I think it's apparent how much simpler the mobile code is than the full site.

So, to summarize: The creation of a mobile Web site, while possible in a number of ways, can be done in a number of distinct steps:

1. Design the mobile CSS file, and decide how the user experience should change on the new device.

2. Insert the HTML that causes the CSS to be called by the mobile device and not by traditional browsers.

3. Test it with as many devices as possible, and edit the CSS where necessary.

If you can perform these steps, then you can create a mobile-specific site that will benefit your users without any input from them.

Outside Services for Mobilization

A few online services will "mobilize" your existing Web site for you, stripping it of any extraneous images and such and presenting it to the end user on a mobile device in a more usable form. The largest of these is a service by Google that it seemingly doesn't advertise, known as Google Mobile Optimizer (http://www.google.com/gwt/n). You enter your Web site's URL, and then Google provides you with an optimized site with a separate URL that you can advertise to patrons. It isn't nearly as good as building your own mobile pages with a separate CSS file, but in a pinch it does work for devices with less-than-full browser experiences. These sites provide a similar service:

▶ Skweezer: www.skweezer.com

▶ IYHY: www.iyhy.com

▶ Usablenet Assistive: http://transcoder.usablenet.com/tt

Give them a try, and see if they provide you with a "good enough" user experience. Any mobile access is better than no mobile access for your patrons!

▶ MAKE YOUR OPAC MOBILE

Libraries have another major online resource that patrons must access that is usually separate from their Web site proper: the OPAC. While many have argued for the destruction of the very term OPAC (online public access catalog: it's a pretty dated acronym at this point), unfortunately we don't have anything better to call it yet, so we'll have to stick with it here. What do we mean when we say Mobile OPAC? The OPAC is accessible and usable from a mobile device. It's possible that, just like your Web site, the regular Web version of your OPAC is perfectly usable on phones. But it isn't likely for most of the smartphones out there, and it can still be a huge help for your patrons to have a mobile-specific version.

Unfortunately, library OPACs are, with very few exceptions, particularly hard to modify in significant ways. Because they are vendor driven for the most part, and are closed source, the OPACs of most libraries are difficult to modify in any significant way, including making them more friendly for mobile browsers. Only one major integrated library system (ILS) vendor offers a mobile version of its OPAC software (Innovative Interfaces' AirPAC product), and a quick search around the Web identifies only a handful of libraries that offer a mobile OPAC to their patrons. Ed Vielmetti, on his blog Superpatron (http://vielmetti.typepad.com/superpatron/2008/05/mobile-versions.html), identified less than two dozen libraries offering mobile OPACs, and that was with the help of his readers in the comments. I would like to believe that this low number relates to how difficult it is to make the catalog mobile, but it is always possible that it speaks to priorities and to the fact that libraries haven't yet been asked to make their catalogs more accessible on the mobile phone. I think this is going to change.

Innovative Interfaces' AirPAC appears to be the most popular mobile-specific OPAC add-on for their Millennium ILS. My research and questioning turned up no other commercial ILS with a specifically mobile aspect to its OPAC offering. Of course, some enterprising librarians have managed to make their OPACs mobile friendly anyway. Let's take a look at a few of them.

North Carolina State University (NCSU) wrote its own mobile interface, and you can tell the thoughtfulness that it exhibits toward its users (see Figure 3.3). It includes not only the basics like a catalog search but also useful additions like a link to see if there are computers available for use in a lab, library hours, a searchable campus directory, and even a link to public transit information. NCSU's results pages are clean, and while it made the decision to

▶ Figure 3.3: North Carolina State University's Mobile Web Site (www.lib.ncsu.edu/m)

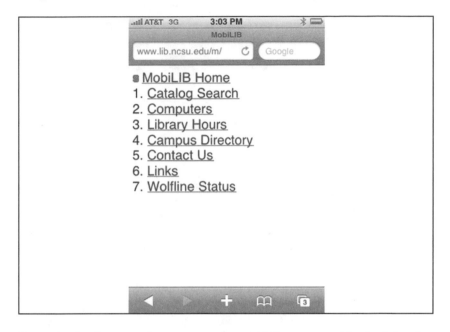

forgo including any images on the mobile pages, this decision increases the number of devices that the interface is usable on. This would work on practically any device with Web access without regard to type of screen, resolution, or other limitations.

Nashville Public Library is another user of Innovative Interfaces' AirPAC (see Figure 3.4). It is purely an OPAC interface, without the larger set of links to other information that the NCSU solution has, but for searching the catalog it works well. It also has the ability for users to log in and check the status of their own accounts. Nashville Public Library also eschews images, which, as noted above, makes the page far more flexible for display on older devices.

One of the best of the mobile interfaces I've seen is Ball State University's. It truly took its Web site and made it as mobile as possible. It includes the OPAC but also mobile-friendly links to news sources like Google News, a title search for journals, links to descriptions of its collections, and direct links to video resources. It does include small graphics, but none of them is integral to the interface. It would still be imminently usable without them (see Figure 3.5).

▶ Figure 3.4: Nashville Public Library AirPAC (http://waldo.library.nashville.org/airpac/jsp/airpacIndex.jsp)

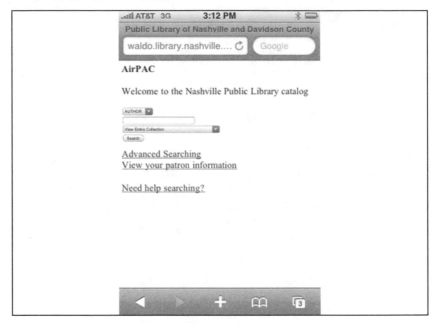

▶ Figure 3.5: Ball State University's Mobile Web Site (www.bsu.edu/libraries/mobile)

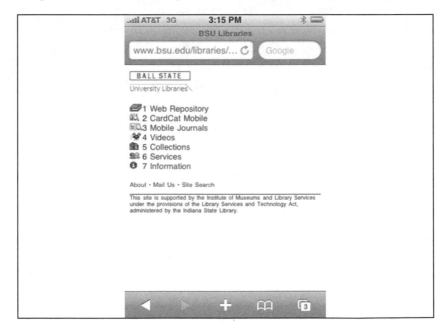

Beyond the amazing work that libraries are doing to make their collections available via mobile, the Massachusetts Institute of Technology (MIT) has taken mobile to a whole new level. Several years ago, MIT made it a priority to develop a framework for mobile development that allowed for the maximum amount of real-time information to be delivered to mobile devices. From their Web site (http://mobi.mit.edu), you can search their directory, see live shuttle and bus schedules, see events happening on campus, get information about courses that you are enrolled in (live information that is updated by the professors), and much more. It is truly mobile accessibility done on a whole different level from other institutions of higher learning (see Figure 3.6).

Even more impressive, MIT has open sourced the code for its mobile development framework (http://sourceforge.net/projects/mitmobileweb), making it available for anyone to use on a mobile Web site (see Figure 3.7). While several universities are beginning to use the MIT framework, I am aware of only one library directly using it, North Carolina State University. In addition, the library mobile vendor Boopsie (www.boopsie.com) provides a hosted op-

▶ Figure 3.6: MIT Web Site, View from Mobile Browser (http://m.mit.edu)

▶ Figure 3.7: MIT Web Site, View from Desktop Browser (http://mobi.mit.edu/about)

tion for libraries looking to move into the mobile space, and one of their options uses the MIT mobile framework.

▶ CREATE PORTABLE INSTRUCTIONAL RESOURCES

Besides offering already-existing library content on a mobile platform, create new resources for instructional and reference use. Text resources can be treated just like the rest of a Web site and converted to mobile with some CSS magic. The really interesting reference and instructional materials these days are driven by audio and video content: podcasts, screencasts, video capture of classes, narrated slideshows, and more. How do you get started developing these sorts of materials for mobile use, and how do you distribute them to the world? This section will give you the basics as well as go into detail about how best to get them out and into the mobile world.

First, a caveat: Entire books have been written on creating podcasts, screencasts, and videos for instructional use. There is no chance that I can cover in this section everything there is to know about these subjects. Instead, the goal is to give you sort of a 10,000-foot view of them, painting in broad strokes how to proceed if you're just getting started. While I may mention specific applications, it is only out of familiarity and not because they are the only way to handle the media in question. I will give several applications where I can and identify them by level of difficulty.

Creating Audio Content

Creating and distributing audio content online has come to be generically called "podcasting," although it isn't necessary to have an iPod to enjoy them. Podcasting refers to the use of an RSS feed to transport an audio file in an automated fashion so that content can be subscribed to and updated without interaction by the patron. Understanding the basic steps, from creation to consumption, will give you the road map you need to get started generating audio content for mobile devices.

At its most basic, creating audio on a computer takes a microphone and some software. If you are capturing audio in a controlled environment, like a closed office, some form of external microphone will increase the quality of your audio a great deal. For most desktop captures of audio, just about any headset microphone will give you very clear sound and will plug directly into the "Audio In" port on your computer via a minijack connector. Slightly more expensive, and just a tiny bit more complicated, is a USB microphone like the Blue Snowball, which plugs into the "USB" port of your computer and is selectable in the audio settings of your system. The truth is that while you can spend an enormous amount on a microphone, and it is true that there is a relationship between price and quality, even a very, very inexpensive microphone is enough to get you started capturing audio.

For the software piece of the puzzle, I highly recommend the open source Audacity. Audacity is an audio editor that allows capturing and editing of multitrack audio, and it will import and export from a number of common formats, including (with the addition of the also open source LAME codec) MP3. You can use Audacity to record the input from your microphone, edit it, and then export the finished audio for distribution, and the best part is that Audacity is free and available for all major computer systems (Windows, Mac, and Linux). There are other options, of course. Windows has a ton of basic audio options, lots of them free, and if you purchased an Apple computer in the past few years it came with GarageBand, an excellent audio program. But even though I use a MacBook, and have GarageBand, I most often find myself using Audacity to do basic audio capturing.

Once captured, there are some basic audio edits that you can do in order to help improve the listenability of your audio. Keep in mind that the end product of audio for a podcast is almost always going to be an MP3 file. MP3s are a highly compressed audio filetype and use a "lossy" form of compression where audio information is actually removed from the file in order to make the file as small as possible. The information removed is determined by a complicated algorithm, but the data loss typically doesn't affect the listenability of the audio in any serious way, especially for the purposes of capturing voices talking. As a matter of fact, you can drop the sample rate of an MP3 way down to make the file smaller for voice; most voice podcasts that I listen to settle for 64 kbps encoding, which sounds great with just voice. If you were listening to more sonically complex audio, like most music or singing, 64 kbps would sound horrible. You need the extra sampling rate of 128 or 192 kbps at least for music to sound good.

With Audacity, you can set the quality of the MP3 when you export it, but, like other lossy file types, you don't want to re-encode it time and again. This means not opening the file, editing, exporting, then reopening, editing, and re-exporting over and over. If you do that, you will start to hear a degradation in the sound. So do your editing on the audio before you down sample it into a lossy format.

Once you've produced your audio content, the next step is distribution. As a podcast is just an RSS feed with an enclosure for some sort of content, there are several easy ways to get your audio out to your audience. The best is probably to use some sort of blog software that will generate the RSS for you with the right sort of enclosure simply by linking to an online MP3 player. If you have access to a server, the open source version of WordPress is absolutely the software I recommend for this. If you are at all familiar with blogs and blogging you can have your podcast up and running in a matter of minutes. One of the strengths of WordPress is its plug-in system, which allows users to extend the functionality to their liking by downloading and installing a variety of plug-ins. There are two that are crucial for podcasting using WordPress, and if you go this route you would be well served to choose one of these to help you with maintaining your podcasts.

The first plug-in is PodPress (www.podpress.org), which will allow you to add metadata to your podcast, will manage your media for you, and will automatically handle the updating of your iTunes feed if you'd like to use this functionality. It is used by a lot of library podcasts and by the Library Information Technology Association (LITA) for its podcasts on litablog.org.

The second plug-in for WordPress that I recommend is PowerPress (www.blubrry.com/powerpress). Its list of features is at least as long as PodPress's, but it's a newer entry into the plug-in fight, and it is a bit more modern in the way that it deals with the WordPress interface. It will also allow for import of settings from PodPress, if you wish to move to PowerPress but have been using PodPress until now. Both are incredibly useful tools for managing podcasts.

Failing having access to a server (or the ability to pay for one as you go), there are services that will host your blog and your files for free or at a very, very low cost. One example of a hosted service, the hosted version of the WordPress software I mentioned earlier, can be found at Wordpress.com and includes, free, three gigabytes of storage, or enough for about 45 hours of MP3 audio. If you need more at a later point, Wordpress.com will sell you extra space very inexpensively; you can get another five gigabytes of storage (another 75 hours of audio storage, give or take) for $20.00 a year. There are other options available if you look around, but WordPress is a reliable and trusted host for blogs and podcasts.

Now that we have audio and a place for it to live, there are two more steps I would recommend. The first is to take your blog's RSS feed and convert it to a FeedBurner feed. FeedBurner (available at www.feedburner.google.com) is a service that gives you several things, but the best is the ability to directly measure how many people are subscribing to your podcast. Without it, it's a bit harder to get at your RSS feed statistics. You can also get interesting statistics like how people are gathering your feed and what the most popular items in your feed are. FeedBurner gives you the numbers that you need to tweak your podcasts and make them work better.

The other step I recommend is, if you are looking to distribute your podcast widely, to make sure that your podcast is in the iTunes Store. iTunes is the most popular place where people find and download podcasts, and having your podcast listed there is a huge publicity tool. You do have to have an iTunes account to get your podcast into the store, but otherwise it is a quick and easy process. When you log in to iTunes and go to the Music Store, you simply click on the Podcast section. At the bottom of that page is a "Submit a Podcast" link that will walk you through the process. The process isn't any more complicated than typing some information in and copying and pasting your RSS feed URL into a form. Once you complete the sign-up process, Apple will preview your podcast to make sure it is what you claimed it is and then list it in the iTunes Store, available for download and subscription. If you are new to podcasting, there is no better place for your podcast to be listed if you are looking for an audience.

Offering Videocasts

The biggest advantage of podcasts is their automated delivery to patrons. Once patrons subscribe to your RSS feed, they will get any podcast you throw into the feed, without effort or attention. It will show up, and you can keep adding ongoing content simply by posting to your blog. This is as true for video as it is for audio, with the biggest difference being that while MP3 is a standard file format for audio, there isn't quite the same agreed-upon standard for video. The closest we have for a true standard for video is MPEG-4, which will play on nearly all portable video devices. It will also play on most video-capable mobile phones, including the iPhone, BlackBerry, and G1. Not all mobile devices can play video, but in the future it is likely that video will be the norm rather than the exception that it is now.

There are lots of options for video, though, that can be really useful for libraries. You can film library tours, tutorials on how to find things in the library or use specific equipment like microfilm machines, and even screencasts that illustrate online features like databases and your catalog. Again, dealing with the tools necessary to create high-quality video is beyond the scope of this book, but I will mention a few tools with a range of complexity.

For a far more in-depth look at creating video, check out Sean Robinson's *Library Videos and Webcasts*, #4 in this Tech Set series.

For capturing video, you need a camera that has some form of video mode, but it doesn't necessarily have to be a $10,000.00 HD (high definition) camera. For some video capture, it may be that the video mode on your digital still camera is just fine; most of them do basic video capture reasonably well. Or you could get by with something like a Flip Video camera, which will do 720 HD video for around $200.00. You can, of course, spend lots of money on a video camera, and, if you are planning lots of video production you might want to consider investing between $800.00 and $1,000.00 in an HD camera with a good lens from a name brand like Sony or Canon. These decisions will all depend on how much you are planning and how flexible you want the final result. All video compression is lossy in some way. Moving from your original capture down into your distribution will result in some loss of video quality, so the higher the quality you start with, the more you can lose and not notice it.

For editing video, you will need a reasonably powered computer, but nearly anything produced in the past couple of years will do an adequate job for basic video editing. Again, if you are going to be undertaking a huge amount of video work, you will feel the benefit of having a more powerful computer. With video, there is a lot of compression and decompression, and if you are editing in HD (either 720 pixels or 1,080 pixels across) you will end up waiting for the video to render into different formats if you are on a slower machine. Like any interaction with a computer, more RAM and a faster processor will always make things go just a bit faster, and with real video work you can even feel the difference in the speed of the hard drive, which is nearly impossible to notice for day-to-day computer work.

For easy video editing, I'm going to be a bit biased; I think it is really hard to beat the Apple Macintosh and OS X for making video easy to use. You can get started editing video with an entry-level iMac, which comes with the Apple iLife Suite. iLife includes iMovie, a straightforward and powerful video editor that will handle a myriad of video files and give you drag-and-drop options for everything from transitions between scenes to the soundtrack behind the video. iLife also has iDVD, which will allow you to archive your videos to DVD in one step. iMovie itself doesn't do everything; Apple intentionally strips down certain functionalities in order to make the user interface simple. But this does sometimes leave holes in what you may want to do with your video, especially in the realm of special effects. If you want a slow-motion scene, for instance, iMovie doesn't have that as an option, and the same stands for most other sorts of video effects that you might want to use. Nothing else even comes close, though, for ease of use.

iMovie will also allow you to export the video into numerous formats with single-click export to iPhone- or iPod Touch–compatible video.

On the Windows side of the world, the entry-level video editing software is Windows Movie Maker. While not as elegant in user experience as iMovie for the Mac, it is a very functional video editing system and is available as a free download for users of Microsoft XP or Vista. It will allow the importing of the common Windows video formats (AVI, WMV) and editing in a similar way to iMovie, with the ability to cut/crop the video, add and remove audio, and more. Windows Movie Maker will only export, however, into Windows Media formats and not natively into the video format for most mobile phones. If you are editing your video in Movie Maker, you will have to find software that will convert to the appropriate format for you as a secondary measure.

Once you step away from these entry-level editors, there are literally dozens of options at all price ranges. The most popular commercial software for editing video is Adobe Premiere, which is available in both Premiere Pro, the professional version, and Premiere Elements, the consumer version. Premiere Pro is available for both OS X and Windows, while Elements is available for Windows only. On the Apple side of the coin is Final Cut, the equivalent to Premiere. It is also available in both a professional (Final Cut Pro) and a commercial (Final Cut Express) version. The commercial versions of both programs are just slightly less fully featured than the professional, with various high-end capabilities removed. But for 99 percent of users, even the commercial versions of these programs have more features than most anyone is likely to use. And the professional versions are actively used to produce video that you see every day, including television programs and commercials.

Videocasting versus Screencasting

The major difference between what I'm calling "videocasting" and "screencasting" is that with the former you are actually using a camera to capture video, while with the latter you are capturing the screen of your computer itself. The differences between the two techniques may not be obvious at first. We are used to video as a medium and automatically make a lot of decent decisions when we film someone or something; even something as simple as focusing on the face of the person talking might not be obvious if you weren't used to the medium already. Screencasting isn't something with which most people are immediately familiar. It requires a lot of trial and error when you start, especially with things like resolution and font size; making the screen you capture readable for your viewers is much more difficult than you might expect.

Screencasting

We have covered editing existing video, but what if you want to do screencasts? There are a bunch of options when it comes to recording activity on a computer screen, but the market seems to lean heavily on the Windows software side of the divide. The largest market share for screencasting is probably a toss-up between TechSmith's Camtasia and Adobe Captivate. Both are available for Windows, and TechSmith recently released the first Camtasia version for OS X–based systems. Adobe is currently beta-testing a Macintosh version of Captivate but has not announced release date, pricing, or other information. Both Camtasia and Captivate offer a slew of options for screen capture and editing, although some prefer to do the raw capture in one or the other and then edit the video directly with a video editor.

For the Mac, there are a few options for screencasting, even without the two 800-pound gorillas of the Windows side of the world. My two favorites are Screenflick by the Araelium Group and ScreenFlow by Telestream. Screenflick is the less expensive of the two ($29.00 versus ScreenFlow's $99.00) and definitely doesn't have all of the features of ScreenFlow, but it will do a very good job of capturing your screen to video. Screenflick will also output a variety of resolutions and sizes, making editing easier. ScreenFlow is my favorite overall screencast program for the Mac because of its easy-to-use interface and ability to record both video and screen at the same time, giving a lot of flexibility to your final presentation. You can move from a close-up of you talking to the screen and back, with great transitions. It just makes your production look very professional.

The biggest problem when doing screen captures for mobile use is ensuring that text on the screen is still readable after it has been shrunk down to the dimensions of a mobile screen. You're going to be capturing your desktop or laptop screen at, most likely, over a thousand pixels wide and trying to reduce it to just 200 or 300 pixels at most. This level of reduction will render text simply unreadable unless you plan for it early and either reduce your screen resolution while capturing or enlarge the text size proportionally for the capture so that when reduced it will still be readable. Voiceovers will also help to ensure that people can follow along with what you are doing. Screencasts are in some ways harder to deal with than simply filmed video because of the resolution and other issues, but it can be very powerful for students who need a helping hand in searching a database when you aren't available. Most capture programs allow for zooming and "pull outs" of sections of the screen, which also help with legibility at small screen sizes.

The largest unknown at this point in the delivery of mobile video is screen resolution and ratio. Because phones come in different sizes and form factors, and you probably don't have the resources to try to render a separate video at every possible resolution, you will likely be creating video at larger-than-mobile sizes and then using a software tool to render the video down to the appropriate sizes for the most common device sizes. Mobile devices also have different aspect ratios: 3:2, 4:3, 16:9. This is the ratio of height to width for the screen, and it will affect the shape of the video that you view. If you want to specifically develop for a given device, like the iPhone and iPod Touch, that ratio (1.5:1) will result in the video displaying with black bars on the sides of a 4:3 device, for instance. The most common movie ratio now is 16:9, which results in black bars at the top and bottom of the video when displayed on a 1.5:1 device. You may want to shoot for a roughly 4:3 ratio, which will display well on most devices, with just a bit of clipping on the edges. If you really want to focus, though, the mobile phones most likely to be used to watch video (iPhone, G1, BlackBerry Storm, Palm Pre) can all handle 3:2 well.

Once you've produced your screencast, the next step is distribution, just like the audio podcasts. As mentioned earlier, while older mobile devices, especially cell phones, have trouble with video, newer devices have seemingly settled around the MP4 standard for playback. More and more devices are also supporting H.264 encoding.

> *More tech talk:* Video files have both a wrapper, most easily understood as filetype, like MP4 or AVI, and a codec that is used inside the wrapper. MP4 supports multiple codecs, the most recent being H.264, which gives it the highest quality at the lowest size currently possible.

MP4 with H.264 will ensure that you can play on the iPhone, newer BlackBerry devices, and the G1, which covers most smartphones. 3GP is an older video format specifically designed for 3G mobile phones that is a variant of MP4, if you want to distribute two different forms of video to cover the absolute most users you can. But generic MP4 is probably the best option for a single distribution method.

Just like audio, the easiest way to get your video into an RSS feed is to use a blog that will create the feed for you. Another option for video, though, that doesn't really exist for purely audio podcasts, is that there are many ways to distribute your video online and also as a podcast, simultaneously. As one example, a service like blip.tv will host your videos and give you an RSS feed that you can distribute as a podcast feed. The overall problem that you have to solve is where the video lives, because it has to be available on the Web in order for it to be pulled down by a browser. If you have a library server that can act as a file server, just putting the files there and pointing to it via a blog post will accomplish distributing the video. Video files tend to be rather large, though, and can become a management issue as they build up. If you plan on doing regular videos, putting some thought into storage and archiving is a good idea upfront so that you don't find yourself in a year's time with gigabytes worth of videos that you don't know what to do with.

In review, when you move into doing videocasts for mobile devices, it is best to start by concentrating on just one format for your production. MP4 is the most widely used video standard at this point, although it is always possible that the next few years will bring a new standard to light. Concentrate on the quality of the video, especially when it comes to screencasts, and make sure that you keep reminding yourself that the eventual viewer will be seeing the video on a screen much smaller than your monitor. Distribute both on the Web, if possible, and via a blog or other RSS creator. It's easier to describe than to do, but then again, many things are.

▶ OFFER MOBILE LIBRARY TOURS

For lots of librarians, just telling patrons where everything is becomes a normal part of the job. Libraries are usually pretty large buildings, and they aren't normally designed with the end user in mind. At some libraries, providing some form of automated tour relieves a lot of pressure for staff to do large-scale orientation, whether it's for the incoming freshman class at a university or for a visiting high school group. You can automate a tour of your library with mobile devices in one of several ways, but the two most common are through preloaded audio or preloaded video. You can also provide mobile users with downloadable maps and other static forms of orientation. Columbia University (www.columbia.edu/cu/lweb/indiv/butler/floor/index.html) uses this method.

If you are interested in putting together a mobile tour for your library, the best place to start is the same place you would with any other audio or video production: with a script and a storyboard. Take the time to actually walk through your library with fresh eyes and decide what you would like to highlight. Once you've got an outline of the tour, you can script it, writing out everything in a conversational way. For an audio tour, that might be all you need, but if you are doing video, it would be good to take it a step further and do a concise storyboard for important sections of the tour. When you actually start filming, having the notes and a storyboard will make things go much more smoothly and ensure that you get shots that match the script.

It's also during the scripting/storyboarding phase when you can start to see whether your tour should be a single file or multiple, smaller files. If you have a huge building, with lots of details you want to point out, making it one large, long tour might just fatigue your patrons. No one really wants to walk around for 45 minutes listening and watching someone talk about the things that are in front of them without a break. So think about how long you want to have a single piece of the tour and where you can take breaks. Perhaps the different parts of your library are interesting to different patron groups (for instance, students might be really interested in your information commons, but your faculty might want to know more about the Special Collections). If there are easy ways to break the tour up so that it's useful in multiple ways, go for it.

Once you have the script and storyboard, it's time to record! It may take several tries to get the audio you want, and you should really pay attention to pacing and timing. If necessary, walk the tour with a stopwatch, and time out the transitions and such so that you aren't making your poor patrons sprint to keep up with you.

Quick Tips for Video

When we filmed our tour at my place of work, we put together a sort of steady-cam outfit by mounting our camera on a rolling cart and securing it so that we could roll the camera rather than walking with it. It makes the video look very smooth and helps prevent the bouncing that happens no matter how careful you are.

Another tip is to pay attention to signage and highlight the various information points in the library. Don't try to be exhaustive and tell them absolutely everything, at least for the introductory tour.

Sometimes a more focused tour of a specified area or for a specialized audience is worth pursuing. Is there a specific archive or collection of special interest, or is the building interesting not just because it's a library but because it has some historical value? These are great topics for a mobile tour.

For video, because you'll likely be filming as you walk, the timing may come a bit more naturally—you can record while watching the video. Another great idea that several libraries utilize is the addition of "Stop Here!" signage or some other visual cues that let people know where the next stop on the tour is. This makes it far easier for the patrons to know that they are on the right path, especially with audio-only tours.

If you are recording just audio and have decided to keep the tour as a single file, it may still be helpful to break the recording up into sections. It's much harder than you may think to record without mistakes for a long period, even more than just a minute or two. You can always put the files together using Audacity or another audio editor.

Once you have the files recorded, distribution is the same as for other multimedia content. You can push the files out via podcast, but for this you probably want to have downloadable or possibly streaming copies available. Podcasts are for existing patrons, whereas the tour is for new ones. You want a static place where people can go to find the files and where your public service desks can refer people to for download.

A number of libraries have done a particularly good job with producing a mobile tour of their library:

Duke University and the Bostock Library
http://library.duke.edu/about/perkinsproject/audio-tour.html
Duke University includes virtual tours of both the Perkins and Bostock Libraries and also offers a downloadable audio walking tour of the Bostock Library that guides you through the entire building.

Ohio University and the Alden Library
www.library.ohiou.edu/podcasts/?page_id=14
Ohio University has gone remarkably out of the way to make its library friendly by including not only an English audio tour but also tours in seven additional languages, including Mandarin, Swahili, Japanese, and Arabic.

Michigan State University Library
http://guides.lib.msu.edu/page.phtml?page_id=1010

Not only does this library have tours in multiple languages, but they also include the script for the tour as a PDF document. It's a thoughtful touch, and it didn't really take any additional time because the creators had to have the script anyway.

Temple University Library
http://blog.library.temple.edu/liblog/archives/2009/03/new-cell-phone.html
Temple uses a completely different system for their audio tour, one where you use your cell phone natively, call a number, and are fed the audio like any phone call. No MP3 players or downloads involved! This is a service provided by a company called Guide by Cell.

Guide by Cell

The way Temple's system works is that you record your audio, and it gets assigned a phone number and "extension." Inside the library, you list the appropriate numbers (Circulation desk, #1; Reference desk, #2, etc.). When patrons get to each point, they simply dial a phone number, enter the "extension," and hear your prerecorded message. This method has both advantages and disadvantages. It can be asynchronously designed so that people happen upon the informational points serendipitously rather than being guided through the building step by step. It also has more of a "self-guided" feel to it. Of course, the downside is that it is a commercial service and has a price tag attached to it.

▶ OFFER MOBILE COLLECTIONS

When looking at the option of providing access to your collections via a mobile device, what may be easy to provide may not be the thing that your patrons need the most. The easiest portion of your collection to provide to mobile users is, most likely, in your archives. Most libraries with archives have some level of digitization happening, and it's likely that some of the material in question is in the public domain and can be freely shared. Providing access to other materials, especially books, becomes difficult legally. Even if you have digitization equipment, without costly negotiations with publishers for the right to do so, digitizing and providing electronic access isn't allowed by U.S. copyright law for any books published in the past 80 years or so.

However, some libraries have successfully managed to license content for distribution to mobile devices either by going with a specific vendor that provides the service or by dealing with individual publishers to obtain the rights to do so. A number of vendors offer mobile content for libraries, but the two best known are Overdrive and NetLibrary. Both provide audiobooks that are compatible with a large number of devices, and both provide e-books, but the e-book offerings are limited to phones with Mobipocket Reader support for the digital rights management involved. NetLibrary provides some e-books that are compatible with the Sony Reader E Ink device, but it doesn't look like either are as friendly as they could be with mobile devices just yet.

Audiobooks

Many libraries use one or both of Overdrive's and NetLibrary's services to provide audiobooks to their patrons. Overdrive says it has over 100,000 downloadable titles, while NetLibrary claims 190,000 e-books and thousands of audiobooks. Both provide audiobooks in formats not compatible with most cell phones (WMA, or Windows Media files, complete with Digital Rights Management [DRM]), but both do provide MP3 options for music. Overdrive and NetLibrary both allow for the "expiration" of the digital file via the Windows Media DRM settings so that a patron's download will cease working past the due date of the checkout. The much smaller catalog of MP3 files from both publishers are DRM free and will play on any portable music device, including cell phones that are audio capable.

From the patrons' standpoint, the files themselves are downloaded to their computer via one of the services and then must be moved onto their device as a separate step. This isn't terribly inconvenient, but it is one additional step for users to have to go through.

There are free audiobooks available from public domain sources for mobile phones as well as the commercial entities mentioned. One very good option is LibriVox (http://librivox.org). The LibriVox organization is a collection of volunteers who read public domain works into audiobooks and then make them freely available for download in non-DRM, open formats. That means that they are all available as an .mp3 file and are DRM free with no restrictions at all. LibriVox currently has over 2,000 titles available, and all are free. Because they are in the public domain, your library could absolutely download and provide access to these for your patrons, mobile or otherwise.

I have been unable to find anyone delivering streaming audiobooks to mobile users or otherwise bypassing the need for an intermediary download step to a computer. I'm certain that this is coming, as there is increased pressure for most media to be delivered as needed. It is possible to buy audiobooks directly from the iTunes store on the iPhone itself, but they don't stream. It's the traditional purchase, then download, method of obtaining content.

Movies To-Go

Movies are more complicated to offer to the mobile user than just about any other media type. Not only is there, generally speaking, a legal quagmire to ford, but the reality of the sheer size of video as well. Offering either streaming or downloadable video is costly on the server front, needing lots of bandwidth and storage space to make the experience positive for the patron. It is very difficult for an individual library to deliver video media reliably to mobile devices.

This isn't to say there aren't options. Some libraries circulate devices for patrons to watch videos on, where the librarians are digitizing and loading the device and relying on the device itself to be a "locker" for the video files in order to prevent further duplication of the content. One way to do this sort of mobile circulation is to use a device like an iPod Touch that the library itself owns and movies that the library has licensed for digital distribution. Digitizing the movies into an iPod-friendly format is reasonably straightforward using software such as Handbrake. Sync the films, and circulate! This assumes that the library has been able to secure the rights to digitization and limited distribution. I am not aware of any library that has successfully managed this, as the rights clearance and other licensing issues are more difficult and expensive than most libraries are capable of working through.

There are always library vendors attempting to fill the gap for video to-go, and the most successful of these appears to be Overdrive. Overdrive provides video in mobile sizes for download, but only in a DRM Windows Media format. This means that your mobile device has to be licensed by Microsoft to play their particular DRM, which limits you to Windows Mobile devices. There are lots of cell phones running Windows Mobile, however, and Overdrive should work with most of them. Overdrive doesn't advertise an overall title count for their video but are adding titles regularly. Overdrive provides video content from PBS, Magnolia Pictures, Starz, and other video distributors.

▶ PROVIDE SMS SERVICES IN YOUR LIBRARY

Short Message Service, or SMS, is a common feature available with nearly every mobile phone sold in the past 10 years. Sometimes called texting, or txting, it is a specific way of sending short messages directly from handset to handset. It is a form of person-to-person, asynchronous messaging, limited by protocol to just 160 characters. SMS is, by volume, the most popular electronic communications format in the world, and Wikipedia even calls it "the most widely used data application on the planet" (http://en .wikipedia .org/w/index.php?title=SMS&oldid=282157961). There are estimates as high as 2.4 billion people using SMS, or almost half of the population of the earth. It is by a wide, wide margin the most popular messaging system in the world.

If SMS is so popular, and so many people are using it, there must be libraries using it, and indeed there are. Many libraries use SMS in a variety of ways, with two primary functions related to library services cropping up again and again in libraries of all types: reference and circulation. We'll examine both and take a look at the variety of options in providing these services.

Reference Services

Reference services via SMS are increasingly being provided as the United States catches up to the rest of the world with texting. There are several ways that a reference department can take questions via SMS. The most straightforward of the options is to simply get and maintain a mobile phone for use by reference staff and to publicize that number as a separate contact point for reference questions. You can send and receive messages from the phone just as if it were a private line. There are both advantages and disadvantages to this solution, of course. You can then only use the phone itself to answer and receive messages and can only pass off questions by giving the handset to someone. It is possible, usually via a Bluetooth connection, to connect the phone to a computer and have software on the computer itself act as a bridge for SMS conversations. So a second option, also involving a phone directly, is to tie it to a computer and interact that way. Both of these methods create a separate workflow for SMS reference questions and aren't as streamlined as integrating SMS into an already existing workflow. As well, there are often security issues to be considered, and, depending on how your library handles IM staffing, possible abuse of the phone.

Another option for handling reference questions via SMS involves a sort of a hack (a nonstandard and somewhat backdoor, but not illegal, method) with AOL Instant Messenger. AIM allows you to interact over its network via SMS by doing the following:

▶ Send a text to 246246 with the format of "send <username> message." As an example, the AOL username for my library is utcref, so if someone wanted to send us an SMS asking what time we closed, the message would look like this: "send utcref what time do you close?"

▶ Once the conversation starts in your IM client, it can be treated as if it were a normal IM exchange. From the library's standpoint, it comes in just as any other IM would. It also doesn't matter what client you are using, either: the native AOL, Digsby, Meebo, Pidgin, or any other multiprotocol IM program. In the library, the SMS blends right in with the rest of the IM reference. Little training is required, and the librarians won't have to learn a new tool.

Yet another option is related to the popular library IM service LibraryH3lp (https://libraryh3lp.com). LibraryH3lp is a commercial service that offers library-specific IM reference. According to its "What Is LibraryH3lp?" Web page:

> LibraryH3lp is an integrated web chat/IM system written specifically for libraries. It allows *multiple* librarians to receive chats from its *native chat widget* or Meebo Me widgets as well as IMs from patrons on other IM networks such as AIM, Yahoo!, MSN, Google Talk, ICQ. While it routes messages to multiple librarians, only the first one to respond "wins" the chat and becomes connected with the patron.
>
> It also incorporates an SMS gateway that works using a library-supplied Google Android phone. This allows patrons to text their library using a phone number rather than a short code. Librarians in the same administrative domain can transfer any chats, IMs, or text messages to each other as needed. The system provides an administrative backend for service creation, management, and centralized transcript storage, download, and deletion.

The just-released SMS Gateway application is thus far limited to use by the Android G1. But it gives seamless SMS integration to LibraryH3lp and also requires no training beyond what has already been done in order to use LibraryH3lp. Unfortunately, it does require a mobile contract with SMS and maintenance of that contract over time in order to keep the service online, T-Mobile coverage (at least for the time being), and LibraryH3lp. So, while the actual number of libraries this could help is limited, it is a truly elegant solution. Follow these steps to set up the SMS Gateway application:

1. Install a LibraryH3lp program on the G1 itself.
2. Set up the program by giving it a password.
3. In LibraryH3lp, set up the mobile phone as any other gateway, in the same way you would set up another IM protocol.

Now, LibraryH3lp will treat SMS messages coming to the phone just like an IM coming from any other location. You can respond or use any of LibraryH3lp's many functions to deal with the SMS: queue it, redirect it to another user, and more. It allows patrons to text a phone number for the library rather than the AOL short code, bringing a more familiar interaction into the process.

No matter how you incorporate SMS into your reference, your library should be paying attention to texting. CTIA (the International Association for the Wireless Telecommunications Industry) reported that more than 1 trillion (yes, that's trillion, or 1,000 billion) text messages were sent in the United States in 2008 (www.ctia.org/media/press/body.cfm/prid/1811). To put that in perspective, that's almost 32,000 texts a second, every second, day and night, all year. This isn't a technology that will be going away anytime soon and is increasingly central to the information and communication lives of your patrons.

Patron Alerts and Notifications

In addition to the two-way communication of SMS reference services, SMS is ideal for broadcast services as well. If your library sends out notices to its patrons, having the ability to send SMS alerts is a nice alternative to e-mail and much more useful for most younger patrons. Research has shown that the current generation of students sees e-mail as old and outdated; they rely almost exclusively on texting to communicate with each other. There are ILS systems that provide a direct SMS gateway option and natively send texts out to patrons. But even if an ILS doesn't have SMS capabilities built in, it probably has e-mail, and, with a little effort, you can give most patrons, at least in the United States, the option of receiving info via an e-mail SMS gateway.

Most cellular carriers have a gateway that allows e-mail to be transmitted to a mobile phone via SMS. In order to correctly format the e-mail address, you do need both the patron's cell number and the carrier's name, because the syntax changes from carrier to carrier. A full list of these addresses can be found at Wikipedia on the "List of carriers providing SMS transit" page (http://en .wikipedia.org/wiki/List_of_carriers_providing_Email_or_Web_ to_SMS). But the most common carrier formats in the United States look like this:

AT&T: *number*@txt.att.net

Verizon: *number*@vtext.com

Sprint: *number*@messaging.sprintpcs.com

T-Mobile: *number*@tmomail.net

If your ILS can send out alerts via e-mail, you just need to give it the equivalent e-mail address for a patron's cell phone, and it should work transparently. There is still the 160 SMS character limit for transmitting text, so, if your e-mails tend to be very wordy or have extraneous text (signatures and such), you will need to pare them down before implementing SMS in your ILS. If you do send an e-mail through one of these gateways and exceed the 160-character limit, most will break your message across texts. A 500-character e-mail would be delivered in four SMS messages sent sequentially by the gateway. The biggest issue is that often people pay for SMS messages individually on their particular cell plan. If implementing texting in this way, you need to be very clear with your patrons about how many messages they are likely to get. Otherwise, they could be surprised by the number of messages they receive, and, if they are paying per message, it's not a surprise you want them to have.

Another way to reach patrons via SMS is to enroll in one of the many different services that allow you to manage the equivalent of e-mail listservs for text messaging. A number of companies do this sort of management, but two to get you familiar with the sort of options you may have are Mozes (www.mozes.com) and Broadtexter (www.broadtexter.com).

► EXPLORE OTHER IMPLEMENTATION IDEAS

What are other ways in which cell phones might be used in a library? What could a smartphone do in a library setting that would be interesting, and what flexibility could it give to existing processes? Several library services could be extended to help patrons and librarians in various ways. The first concept that I'm going to discuss is something that I haven't seen implemented yet, but certainly it is within the realm of existing technologies. It is taking self-checkout to its logical extension: Self-Check by Mobile.

The implementation that I have in mind is reasonably straightforward, even if it works well only for libraries that have converted to RFID (radio frequency identification). Allow patrons to check books out to themselves using a Web interface with your catalog. When users log in with their library card information, use that to authenticate the checkout and to attach the book to their account. The catalog then needs to tell the security gates that this is a checked-out book and that they don't need to sound the alarm. That's it, really. As long as the Web check-out form is mobile friendly, you can have students checking out their books as they find them on the shelves. The only piece of the puzzle that, to my knowledge, doesn't exist is the connection between the security gates and the catalog. It could also be made to work with an intelligent magnetic desensitizer, if the individual could desensitize a book by simply swiping it and having the security system realize, once more, that the book was checked out via the RFID.

Think of the time saved, both of library staff and patrons. No waiting in line for the patron, and much more time available for your staff. With any mobile browser, on any cell phone, anyone can be a circulation point in your library.

Another potential mobile implementation for libraries is live streaming of video. While it is possible to stream video to laptops and desktops these days with very little effort using Web sites like Ustream (www.ustream.tv) and Stickam (http://stickam.com), streaming to and from mobile devices is still a reasonably new process. Streaming to mobile phones has been available to the larger commercial world for a few years, and various media outlets have streaming services. But Ustream, Stickam, and Qik (http://qik .com) are the first to really put that power into the hands of the average Internet user and easily into the hands of the average library.

All of these Web sites allow any Webcam to stream live to the Web. Libraries are already using live streams to share classes, conferences, and meetings with standard computing equipment. It is just a small step to advertising these events as available on mobile devices. As an example, Ustream has an iPhone application that allows for tuning in to and watching a live stream on your phone over either a WiFi or a 3G connection. Other smartphones can also be used to find these live streams, and, as individuals become more and more used to consuming video over these devices, it may become a standard expectation.

Even more interesting, in just a few short years, video streaming will be standard on phones. Imagine being able to answer questions from patrons by having them show you where in the building they are via a videocam. Directing someone where to find a book on a remote floor of your library becomes much easier when you can follow them via video and let them know where they went wrong.

One of the cornerstones of the new mobile movement will be location-based services. Nearly every new cell phone has within it a GPS chip, capable of pinpointing where you are on the planet to within a few hundred feet. The District of Columbia Public Library iPhone app discussed earlier attempts to show you the closest DC library to you by seeing where you are in the world and passing that information along to Google Maps. But there will be more and more location-based services coming into being, and libraries can help with them in a number of ways. One is by opening your archives to services like Enkin (www.enkin.net) and Layar (http://layar.eu). Both are examples of augmented reality, a metadata overlay for the real world, using your mobile phone's GPS, compass, and camera in a unique way. It allows you to use your phone as a display, showing you what is in front of you, but with a data overlay. Don't know what building you are in front of? Open up Layar, point it at the building, and it will locate you, analyze the building, and then tell you which it is. Now imagine on a university campus, where the archivist has worked to help get the history of the campus buildings into this type of program. Instead of just the building name, you could see the history of the building, timelines of construction, interesting facts, and even pictures of it from different periods. Alumni could use the service to see the campus as they remember it and watch as it changes from then to now.

Now imagine such rich information for areas served by some of our public libraries. Entire towns could be seen, literally, to change before your eyes. This level of data and mobile interaction is happening now, and the possibilities are nearly endless. Libraries have information and data that would be hugely beneficial to these sorts of projects, and we need to be thinking about how we can be a part of this new way of viewing the world.

There are more methods for interacting with your patrons via mobile devices than any one library could implement. No one is doing everything, but it's important that everyone be doing something to reach out to patrons, especially in light of the growth of the mobile phone as the primary computing device in people's lives. Pick one or two things in this chapter, and investigate. See what fits best with your library, your area, and your patrons. Don't be afraid to fail! As Thomas Edison once said, "I have not failed. I've just found 10,000 ways that won't work."

▶4

MARKETING

- ▶ Get the Word Out
- ▶ Promote Open Communication

▶ GET THE WORD OUT

With any shift in the methods that libraries use, we have to think about how those shifts will affect our patrons. This is true even when our patrons are driving the change, because our users have multiple experience levels and a myriad of expectations about the library. The once-a-month patron is different from the once-a-day patron, and we need to take all of the variations into account as we advertise our new capabilities and services. How do we navigate the marketing of the new mobile world?

Several things should be taken into account when thinking about marketing mobile services. Some mobile services, like the availability of a mobile-specific Web site, are best served if they are completely transparent to the patron. The best mobile Web sites are the ones that just work, without any need for the patron to already know anything. If there are issues with automatically sending patrons to a mobile-styled site when they visit with a mobile browser, there obviously needs to be some warning to patrons that said mobile site exists.

It would be nice to only have a link to the mobile site appear if your Web site visitor was actually using a mobile browser, but if you can do that, you should be able to forward them automatically. So we're stuck with a user experience problem: How do you ensure that a mobile user sees the option to click through to a mobile-specific version of your site and in a way that isn't annoying to the majority of those using a traditional computer and browser? Most of the answer will depend on the overall design of the Web site in question. But as a generic answer, one option is to focus on the part of the screen most likely to show up on a low-resolution device, the upper left corner of the page. If you are putting a mobile link anywhere, try to put it there, as anywhere else it is likely to get buried "below the fold" of the display of a low-resolution device.

The other tip for ensuring that people use your mobile site is to keep the URL for the site short and easily typable on a computer keyboard. Save the keystrokes of your users! Which is easier to type: http://mobile.yourlibrary.org, http://yourlibrary.org/mobile, or http://m.yourlibrary.org? Which is easier to remember? Balancing these two features is sometimes difficult, but having an easy-to-use and easy-to-remember URL is a huge bonus for any mobile site.

Aside from making the actual link easy to find and maximizing the use of the URL, traditional advertising works for informing your patrons as to the options they have. Use banners and such on your existing Web site to let patrons know that they have the option of using your site and catalog via their cell phones. Some of them may have never even considered the option, and a simple ad on your site may open up possibilities for them.

It can be more difficult to market services, especially details of services like hours of operation. Marketing is all about immediate effect, not detailed orientation information exchange. But you can get across quite a bit if you try. Think carefully about the amount of information that you really need to get to people. Let them do some of the discovery on their own.

▶ PROMOTE OPEN COMMUNICATION

For services like reference, point-of-need advertising isn't really possible in the same way that it is on the Web. You can, however, ensure that people who approach the desk know that they can contact you via their mobile device. One of my favorite eye-catching pieces of advertising is a small business card with your mobile contact information on it produced by a service like Moo.com. They create really great little cards with just enough room on the back for information about where to find the library via mobile: an SMS number, a Web site address, etc. Moo.com allows you to print a full-color image on one side of the card, so you can theme your mobile cards with pictures of cell phones or other mobile devices to make them easily distinguishable. Really, any sort of take-away card would work; just make sure they are visible and have the appropriate information for the patron. Don't make them, as an example, go to your Web site from the card to get your SMS number. Make the card the only thing they need to contact you in the manner that they wish.

The best way to get the word out about any new service, especially a technologically enhanced service like the various mobile ones, is to use social networks that are already in place. The two fastest growing social networks at the time of this writing are Facebook and Twitter, both of which are perfect for advertising your library and services. While studies have shown that students are especially wary of professors or other administrators on Facebook, there are ways to approach Facebook that won't turn off your "friends."

One way is to create a fan or group page for your library, and highlight services and new library offerings regularly. Fan pages are exactly what the name implies, a page dedicated to something that someone, somewhere, is a fan of. Group pages are for a collection of people interested in a specific topic, subject, or location. Many libraries are using fan pages now that Facebook doesn't allow non-persons to have actual accounts and pages.

> For more information on how to use Facebook in your library, take a look at *A Social Networking Primer for Librarians*, #7 in this Tech Set series, by Cliff Landis.

Aside from maintaining pages in Facebook, you can also buy advertising on the network. Advertising on Facebook is reasonably inexpensive and tends to deliver good results, because the ads are only shown to members of the network that you specify. My place of work has used Facebook advertising with good results for our annual survey, and I can't think of a better way to reach the current generation than through Facebook.

The newest phenomenon on the Web is Twitter, and it's turning into both the place to manage your virtual reputation as a brand and the key starting point for sharing information. Twitter is a form of what's come to be known as microblogging, very short status updates of no more than 140 characters. On Twitter, advertising what you are doing is almost the expectation, especially if you are useful in some way to your followers. Because Twitter is in its very nature a mobile platform (Twitter messages can be set and received via SMS), it is also a great outlet for updating patrons about your mobile endeavors. To some degree you may be preaching to the choir, so to speak, because Twitter users tend to be early-adopters of technology and may be those most likely to have already discovered your mobile services. On the other hand, they are probably the group most likely to use said services, and so reaching out to them can't be a bad thing.

For in-library marketing, consider the possibilities of all of the places where your patrons interact with individuals, with the building, and with the virtual parts of the library. Do you send e-mails for overdue notices and other circulation issues? Add a line in the signature telling patrons that they can get the notices as SMS messages instead. Doing podcasts to supplement your instruction? Make sure that every single class you teach knows about them, and how to access them, and how to check out a device to access them with, if your library provides them. Never underestimate the power of just telling the people at each and every point of contact about your services.

The other marketing trick to keep in mind is that if you know you are going to have some form of serial content, tie them together. Whether this is instructional podcasts that link from one to the other or really any form of continuing content, do teasers from one to the other that point people across the various services you have in order to cross-pollinate and get the maximum amount of notice to all your services.

Also think about promotions that increase the visibility of your mobile services. What would happen if you agreed to wave the first $5.00 in fines of anyone who signed up for SMS messaging to receive overdue notices? Could you drum up interest in a new text reference service by entering everyone who tried it out into a drawing during the first month you offered it? The key is to focus on getting people exposed to the services and hopefully get them talking about them so that they will do the job of promotion for you. A combination of physical advertising, online advertising, and mentioning it directly to patrons will touch all the possible bases and let people know about your new mobile services.

▶5

BEST PRACTICES

▶ **Establish Mobile Reference Services**
▶ **Make Your Services Simple**

Throughout this book I've tried to give positive examples and illustrate what seems to be the common best practices in mobile library development at the current time. In this chapter I'll reiterate some of this advice, but I will also cover common pitfalls and assumptions that can sometimes cause issues with mobile services and development. Along the way, I'll point out resources that can give you a leg up in the production of mobile services and help you understand the mobile space.

▶ESTABLISH MOBILE REFERENCE SERVICES

One of the most common issues relating to mobile services in libraries is the reliance on a traditional desk-time model for services hours. For the purposes of answering questions in person, obviously you must have someone at a desk who is approachable by the patron in question. Once you move to mobile services, whether a reference or some other mobile communication type, you are no longer bound by place or position, only by connectivity. Consider having librarians and staff members monitor mobile reference services, for example, while in their office or at other locations. Where they are isn't important, only how they can be accessed. This is the concept of "roaming reference."

Consider increasing the flexibility of your staffing for mobile services, and see what efficiencies can be gained by distributing virtual services (IM, e-mail, SMS, etc.) across and between multiple staff members. The easier it is for people to hand off a patron interaction, the more flexibility you will have in the way your staff can respond to multiple incoming requests. In this arena, the best solution that I've seen is the LibraryH3lp IM reference system that includes an SMS gateway. It allows for a ridiculous amount of queue management, pushing interactions to other librarians by group or individuals, and generally is designed for the library environment.

Other solutions allow for flexibility in other ways, though. A dedicated SMS reference phone allows for physical handoff of patron interactions by simply handing the mobile phone to someone else. In some situations, there's a lot to be said for centralized reception of an SMS reference service to a dedicated handset. Another benefit of this approach is that statistics become easily trackable, as they become part of the billing process for the phone itself.

One thing to keep in mind is that while I'm suggesting that staff who are involved in SMS and other mobile services can and should multitask, it is very important to keep in mind that they are still manning a "desk" even if said desk is invisible to everyone else. Virtual interactions are often deprioritized in ways that are troublesome, and mobile reference needs to be respected as a patron interaction equal to any other. Indeed, if your library hasn't moved fully into virtual reference services, you may be surprised at your statistics over time. Many libraries are finding that virtual interactions are growing, while in-person reference is slowly shrinking. This is a trend that, with a few outliers, is likely to continue as communication technologies get more and more embedded in daily life. Don't sell either the demand or the difficulty of it short when you begin, and you'll grow the services with fewer issues.

Your decisions about which type of SMS service to use and how to structure it will likely be based on existing staffing and budget limitations. With this in mind, the best practice I can recommend is to ensure that however you choose to enter this new world of library service interaction with patrons, do so with as much ease of use and intuitive interface as possible. The early implementations of IM reference in libraries that insisted on having patrons interact with librarians by going through a specific portal weren't nearly as successful as those that allowed the patrons to interact through the IM services they were already using. In turn, this has less impact than the IM reference service that relied on embedded widgets that required no prior IM knowledge at all. Transparency to the end user is the highest ideal a new service can aspire to.

▶ MAKE YOUR SERVICES SIMPLE

The importance of transparency in design and interface goes triple when it comes to mobile applications and Web sites. There is little more important with interface design (which is, at bottom, a large part of what you are doing when you design a Web site) than making the interaction between patron and information intuitive and thoughtless. Make every decision that your patron has to make blindingly obvious, and try to anticipate as much as you can the most likely decisions that they will make, and make them first. Are you implementing a mobile catalog search? Make sure that your default search is the type that will actually help your patrons the most, and take a look at existing statistics to try and determine this. Don't make your patrons make choices that they shouldn't have to make in the first place. Don't just copy the interface of the existing site unless there is absolutely no option for you to make changes. Optimize the experience for the mobile device as much as possible.

Optimization can be limited when it comes to Web-based interfaces, but if you are writing a native application for a mobile device there is no excuse for just moving an interface directly from an existing service. One of the huge benefits of writing a native application is the flexibility you have, and the potential for really customizing every piece of the interaction, from interface to the management of back-end processes. As an illustration of the importance of interface design, consider the success of the iPhone. It isn't the most powerful phone on the market, and it lacks some basic features that other phones don't (high-resolution camera, autofocus, A2DP Bluetooth, video recording). But it is currently the darling of the mobile phone world because it has an amazing user interface that is completely intuitive, enough so that my 17-month-old daughter can use it. If you can come within any distance of this level of user interface, your patrons will flock to your (mobile) doors.

With either a Web-based mobile site or a dedicated application, it is always a best practice to test more than just internally. No matter how much you try to objectively test your new site, you can't possibly approach it from anything like the perspective of a patron. You and your staff bring with you hundreds of small habits and pieces of knowledge that are gained from working in the library and from dealing with the library-specific tools all the time. When you are ready to show someone the fruits of your mobile labors, get some actual patrons to help you evaluate and iterate the tools. It is much, much harder to effectively test usage procedures and evaluate the user interface than it initially appears for the same reason that library staff make poor subjects: You know what to do, and watching someone make other-than-optimal decisions while using your tool brings out the worst sorts of "just do it this way" behavior. So, a few tips on testing usage procedures:

▶ Always videotape your test subjects. You will find out more about your interface the fifth time you watch their behavior than the first four times combined.

▶ Give generic tasks that don't require advanced knowledge of the interface—don't lead the witness.

▶ Base your questions on actual patron usage, not on what your librarians think is patron usage. While your librarians are certain that patrons always use Library of Congress subject headings to find books on indigenous tribes in Latin America, your search statistics probably say something else.

▶ Don't bother testing more than five to six patrons. More than this clouds results, and less than this may not give you enough information to judge.

▶ Take all feedback from your testers as an opportunity, not as a challenge. Yes, even if they hate it. Especially if they hate it.

Something to consider when developing your mobile Web site is that navigation is different on a mobile device. Most mobile phones don't have the equivalent of a "mouse," where you have a pointer that interacts with links. Instead, most mobile browsers use a scroll-through-links metaphor for navigation, with just a simple D-pad for moving the focus of the browser around. You shouldn't design a mobile site with any need to use a mouse if you want to reach the highest possible number of users.

The other big no-no for a mobile site is an overreliance on high-resolution photographs. Keep in mind that your users are going to be interacting with the site on a device that has a resolution between 100 and 480 pixels wide, and there's just not much room for graphics. As well, the connectivity will range from 802.11 WiFi speeds all the way down to second-generation cellular data networks like EDGE. You don't want to overwhelm the connection with too many pictures. Delay in loading is one of the main reasons that users navigate away from pages, and on a cellular network you may be talking about sub-dial-up speeds. You can definitely include a reasonably sized logo and such, but relying on graphics to drive the mobile version is almost certainly worth reconsidering.

As well, if your site has a lot of advanced multimedia going on (Flash animation, audio or video embeds from other sites, etc.) it may not translate well to a mobile experience. It may be necessary in an extreme case to actually code a completely separate site just for mobile users. But hopefully through following Web standards you can avoid this amount of duplication of effort.

The other set of best practices that I'd like to talk about are the ones I mentioned earlier in the book, having to do with managing change. Libraries of all types are, typically, change resistant. Any bureaucracy is change resistant by its very nature, and libraries have been, historically, seen as a place of stasis, a storehouse or warehouse. In these circumstances, opening up what may be for many libraries a completely new service paradigm can be a complicated process. Follow general best practices for any sort of institutional change, but make sure you include plenty of advanced planning. Provide training where necessary, and, when you believe there may be significant resistance, try and convince with statistics. There are plenty of existing statistics that bolster the claim that the mobile realm is one that libraries ignore at their own peril. There are many ways to overcome political and organizational difficulty, including "trials" of services that work to prove their worth and the use of peer institutions as models to convince the powers-that-be of the wisdom of the new services. Just remember the old saying: you catch more flies with honey than with vinegar.

►6

MEASURES OF SUCCESS

▶ **Track Services**

▶ **Ask Questions**

After all the effort, after convincing your staff to move into this new and somewhat scary mobile world, and after giving these wonderful new capabilities to your patrons . . . how do you know if you succeeded? What can you actually look at to know whether you're moving in the right direction? This chapter addresses how to judge your success and how to build off of one success and into another.

▶TRACK SERVICES

When you begin a new service, one of the things that should always be taken into account is how you will track it. For the purposes of a mobile Web service, like providing a mobile-optimized version of your site, you can use a variety of methods of tracking Web site hits and visits. One method of analyzing Web traffic is to use a software tool to parse the logs on your server to look at traffic patterns and see where your visits are coming from. Most sites have moved away from this method of tracking traffic and instead use something like Google Analytics or another JavaScript-based tracking Web site. Google Analytics is really the market leader for this service, and most others are set up similarly, so explaining how to use Google Analytics will answer many questions about the other sites as well.

To use Google Analytics you need an account with Google. If you don't have a preexisting one, go to www.google.com/analytics and create a new account. Once you've created an account, you will be shown a set of code that looks like this:

```
<script type="text/JavaScript">
var gaJsHost = (("https:" == document.loca-
    tion.protocol) ? "https://ssl." :
    "http://www.");
document.write(unescape("%3Cscript src='" +
    gaJsHost + "google-analytics.com/ga.js'
    type='text/javascript'%3E%3C/script%3E"));
</script>
<script type="text/JavaScript">
try {
var pageTracker = _gat._getTracker("YOUR CODE
    HERE");
pageTracker._trackPageview();
} catch(err) {}</script>
```

This little bit of JavaScript then gets put into the code of the pages you want to track, preferably in the footer or some other easy-to-locate place. It doesn't render in a browser, but what it does is ping the Google servers every time someone loads the page with the code on it. The code grabs a ton of information about the visitor: type of operating system, type of browser, screen resolution, where they came from on the Web, how long they stuck around on your site, and much more. To access all of this information, you simply log on to the Google Analytics page and look through the reports.

One of the huge advantages of Google Analytics is that you can add viewers to the statistics. If you're in a situation where your dean or department head wants to see statistics on a given schedule, you can simply add this person to the account as a viewer, and he or she can check the stats anytime.

Google Analytics will quickly and easily let you track visitors to your site, and, via the browser and screen resolution tracking, it will let you know how many of them are visiting from mobile devices. It's a fast and easy way to understand who, when, and how individuals are hitting your Web site. It's a direct measure of the success of any addition to your site, including mobile access.

As to what constitutes success, that's a measure that you and your team will have to determine. How many hits on the mobile site before you consider it a success? It's probably best to think about the number in terms of a percentage of total visitors to your library Web site. The actual percentage in question will likely be determined by your patron types. Are you the center of a wired and connected community as the public library? Or are you part of a small liberal arts college? In the former case, you might consider "success" to be something in the 2 to 5 percent range at first. In the latter you might be satisfied with less than 1 percent of visitors coming in via mobile. But that's up to you to decide. The tool is there for you to be capable of measurement, at the very least.

How do you measure success for a new public service like text reference? As with raw site visits, there is something to be said for simply analyzing contact statistics. Tracking the raw number of people who try the service out is the place to start. One of the benefits of using a dedicated phone for text reference is that most cellular service providers itemize your text messages on the bill each month, making tracking of by whom and how often the service is being used very easy. This does force you to track the service on a monthly delay, however, and some may want to have a real-time record of the patron texting interactions. For this, you will have to resort to a secondary recording system. Whether it is paper based or computer based is up to your particular statistical methodology.

Determining the level of success for text reference is similar to judging the success of any reference service: How many people do you reach, and how many questions can you answer? Most libraries have experience tracking other sorts of virtual services (IM/chat reference and e-mail reference), and the success level for text will be on the same scale. There is a direct correlation between the amount you advertise a new service and the number of people who know about it, which of course is related to the number who will use it.

Find appropriate advertising spots for your text reference service, and make sure that you cross-promote your services, especially the mobile ones. Make sure that if you have a mobile Web site, it mentions your text reference service, for instance. It is hard to measure the effect of advertising, but you can certainly measure the before and after of a particular advertisement. Take a look at the number of text reference interactions before you start a new campaign and then again after. Measure the week before you start a campaign, the week a campaign runs, and then ongoing so that you can see the effect that a given type of ad has on your services.

▶ ASK QUESTIONS

More difficult than measuring the popularity of a new service is measuring its effectiveness. That is, how useful is the service to your patrons, and how valuable is it to them? It's the difference between measuring the number of students in a class and what it is they are learning. Teachers and instructors have tried for years to find better ways to measure such abstract concepts, and there is no perfect answer, unfortunately. One option is to actively poll patrons at regular intervals and ask them directly how useful the service is to them. If you do a regular library survey, this is the sort of question that should be added in order to try and measure usefulness.

Take a moment to reflect on the myriad of ways that you can take stock of the success of your mobile programs and services. No one way is perfect, but any measurement is better than no measurement.

CONCLUSION

Technology, more than most aspects in libraries, is a huge moving target. We've got formalized procedures for formats that have been around for a century or more, but even after a couple of decades of increasingly digital services and information we're still working out the best processes for them. The next five years are going to bring more frequent and radical change than the previous 20 put together, and a lot of the change is going to be focused on mobile technology. As technology shrinks, individuals are becoming more and more used to truly personal technology; the mobile phone is one of the very few objects that most people carry with them every day, without fail. It becomes an identifiable part of the person, and patrons are very shortly going to be used to the mobile as their first object of inquiry for immediate information needs.

To revisit my William Gibson quote from earlier, the future is already here, it's just not evenly distributed. So, where is the future of the United States being created? In places like Japan, Korea, and Denmark, and in developing nations around the world. Let's take a brief look at the through-the-looking-glass world of mobile phones in Japan, and we can see bits and pieces of where our future might lay.

▶ GLOBAL MOBILE TECHNOLOGY—JAPAN

The term for mobile phones in Japanese is "keitai denwa," and they are typically called just keitai. Keitai are such an integral part of modern Japanese life that there are more services and functions relating to mobile phones there than nearly anywhere else in the world, and they have a dizzying array of phone models and types. They are such an integrated part of the culture that there are media types revolving around keitai specifically, like the keitai shosetsu, or mobile phone novel. Many of the bestselling novels in Japan over the past several years have been written entirely on a cell phone, and one of the most popular Web sites in Japan is a social site dedicated to the distribution of keitai shosetsu (Maho I-land).

Many components of the mobile services in Japan are unique, including the fact that the major carriers use a cellular protocol (W-CDMA) that is largely incompatible with the rest of the world. This makes the mobile hardware in Japan mostly useless in the rest of the world (although this is changing rapidly, and more and more manufacturers are producing phones with radios that play well with other carriers).

Japan's mobile technology is seen as the best in the world because of the incredible variety of services offered to or via a mobile phone. Here's a short list (according to Wikipedia) of the tasks you can do with a cell phone in Japan:

► Send and receive e-mail
► Receive live video feed via Piconet
► Play mobile games, such as the role-playing games Dragon Quest and the Final Fantasy series
► Send and receive instant messages
► Record and play back voices, music, images, and pictures
► Listen to music (functions as an MP3 player)
► Watch videos (functions as an MP4 player)
► View online Flash videos (YouTube, Nico Nico Douga, etc.)
► Send and receive video calls
► Navigate by GPS
► View and listen to TV (1seg) and radio (FM/AM)
► View video-on-demand contents

Cell phones in Japan also have some pretty sophisticated features:

▶ Crime prevention buzzer (with an automatic reporting system to the police)

▶ Pedometer

▶ "Read aloud" system

▶ Fingerprint/face recognition system for the protection of personal data

▶ E-money services, from credit cards to vending machines

From the perspective of a U.S. user of mobile phones, the ability to make video calls or to watch live television seems like science fiction, and, while some electronic money systems are slowly making their way onto U.S. phones, it will be years before we can walk up to a vending machine and reliably pay with our mobile device. In Japan, you can pay for items via your mobile phone (whatever you buy is just charged to your mobile bill), and, because Japan has also moved fully into QR codes, you can make physical objects interact with the mobile world.

However, as advanced as the Japanese cell phone market is, it is possible that the U.S. market may diverge somewhat in development. Rollout of services tends to be much slower in the United States, as geographically it is much more challenging to cover adequately. Not only this, but commuting patterns and other sociological issues have driven the Japanese market in a direction not likely to be exactly copied by the United States. However, the underlying technology and capabilities of Japanese hardware and infrastructure will almost certainly see some uptake here, especially services like video calls.

▶ PREPARING FOR THE NEXT FIVE TO TEN YEARS IN MOBILE

The next five to ten years of mobile development will be focused in, I believe, three main areas: location-based services, personally networked devices, and ubiquitous connectivity. The normal sorts of technological change will continue, and Moore's law will ensure that devices get more and more powerful and less and less expensive. While today the iPhone and its ilk are expensive, running several hundred dollars (unsubsidized by cell phone contract, the iPhone retails for almost $800.00), in ten years we can expect the same level of technology to cost 10 percent of this or less.

When technology of this level is the low end, the high end will be extraordinary, with broadcast-quality cameras and hybrid OLED/E Ink screens that can be read in the dark or in full sunlight. All phones will be extremely location sensitive, knowing where in the world they are at all times and able to use that information to deliver information to the users about nearly any aspect of their surroundings. Libraries have already lost the quick reference battle to Google and the Web. The sorts of questions that were once difficult for the individual to find the answer for ("What year did Catherine the Great die?") are now less than trivial. How will the mobile world change our scope?

Services will be moved out and become fractured. The current services that libraries offer to patrons will change distinctly in a ubiquitous connectivity world. The core services of most libraries, circulation and reference, have the potential to be distributed to point-of-need services that are no longer attached to a physical space. If we move toward the distributed circulation model that I propose in Chapter 4, for most transactions there is no longer the need for staff interaction with a patron for checkout. This is the case already in libraries with self-check machines, but, with the mobile checkout model, you don't have any centralized location for checkout at all. Patrons can check items out to themselves while standing in the stacks, which means that they may never see your checkout desk. Libraries won't be able to completely do away with contact points of some type, however, as there will always be problems with any system that you implement, whether it's on the item end or on the Web end.

Reference services will increasingly move to the mobile interface over the next five to ten years. It wouldn't surprise me in the least to see more and more libraries moving to having a reference-specific mobile device, whether it is a phone like the G1 or a mobile-capable ultra-mobile PC like the Nokia N800. These devices will serve as both a consolidation point for reference interactions (voice, IM, SMS) and a conduit for these interactions to smoothly move from the PC to roaming and back. Via Bluetooth connections, mobile communications can be transferred to a PC, and when staff switch shifts the device moves from person to person, seamlessly transferring the ongoing conversations with it. With this change comes a decreased reliance on place such that a librarian could be effectively manning a virtual desk from anywhere. This is already the case today with IM and e-mail reference, but add voice and SMS to the package, as well as video chat via mobile, in the very near future, and you end up with a very robust set of communication tools for a reference interaction in the palm of your hand.

▶ LOCATION, LOCATION, LOCATION

Location-based services are on a huge upswing currently, and within our time every mobile device is going to be GPS enabled. When you combine global positioning with ubiquitous Internet, you get some very interesting emergent services. Libraries have an opportunity to be an important part of this infrastructure if we can find ways to continue to assert our relevance at a hyperlocal level. Most of this interaction may be completely virtual. Imagine a typical information interaction that might involve a library (since we're already out of the ready-reference business). Patrons will find a book in a bookstore, or read about a book online, and wonder where they can find a copy. They will pull up their mobile device, which knows where they are in the world, and search for the title of the book in their favorite search engine. The search provider should be able to tell which libraries own the book and identify which is closest. Furthermore, the search provider will check availability and show the patrons where the closest copy is that they can actually check out.

Even better is the world that could exist if our database vendors could agree on a geolocation standard for licensing of content. Imagine being able to authenticate a "patron" of your library by geographic location automatically and in the background. Licenses for public libraries would still be based on population, but you would eliminate the need for the patron to initiate a connection with the library prior to being able to access databases. Instead of needing to get a library card in order to prove that you have a mailing address within the city limits, your device would know that you were physically within the city limits and simply allow you access automatically. Your user base would truly be the people in your area, and only in cases where people within the limits were traveling would they need some other form of authentication.

As I mentioned in an earlier chapter, there are location-based services that can and will benefit from library archives. The local history of a town, county, state, or university has an incredible amount of value, especially when put into a localized framework. This is another way that libraries can be active in the development of mobile information. It is not necessarily a direct service that libraries themselves will offer, but nevertheless it is a valuable place for libraries to insert themselves. Providing an open set of historical data to mobile software may become an interesting way for the library to serve both the local community and the larger community of scholars.

A New Kind of Bar Code

One feature that is coming to the United States, and is already popular around the rest of the world, is the type of bar code known as the QR Code (see Figure C.1). This printed two-dimensional bar code is readable by the cameras on most cell phones, and lots of modern phones have the ability to take a picture of the code, translate it, and then display the information it contains. This information is normally a URL that the phone then uses to pull up a Web page.

QR Codes allow you to tag physical objects (like, say, books), and users can interact with a virtual object (any URL you wish). This opens up a lot of possibilities, including the ability to link books with public domain copies to their online counterparts. Users could pick up the physical copy of *Pride and Prejudice* on your shelf, take a picture of the QR Code with their cell phone, and instantly be able to read the book on their phone via Google Books (or Project Gutenberg, or Feedbooks, or any one of a dozen other providers).

▶ Figure C.1: QR Code

Other physical/virtual links can be exploited with QR Codes. Have a large and confusing building for patrons to navigate? Put QR Codes on the walls at specific points, and people can use their cell phones to see a map of the area. Put codes on business cards for your staff members that point to their online contact pages. Anywhere you can think of where a link between the physical world and virtual might be beneficial, the QR Code has the potential to bridge that gap.

All Information Seeking Will Be Mobile

Ready reference went the way of the dodo with the advent of the Internet and the ease with which Google indexes and ranks the mass of information contained within the World Wide Web. Factual questions simply don't get asked as they used to. Once mobile connectivity truly saturates the whole country as it has the metropolitan areas already, patrons will have the Internet at their fingertips regardless of where they happen to physically be. When this happens, services like reference and instruction will need to reexamine their passivity in providing their expertise to patrons. In the current model, with the exception of communicating with interested parties, librarians typically deliver services like reference and instruction by having the patrons come to them to ask a question or sit in a class. This won't be the case for very much longer.

It is already the case that one of the social norms springing up on services like Twitter is to simply ask a question of, in effect, no one (or, depending on how you look at it, everyone). Libraries will need to start actively monitoring the social Web for problems in the same ways that commercial entities are today. The model will likely become some form of monitor and respond rather than wait and answer. Libraries will have to have a presence in the larger social networking arenas and will have to set up an RSS or other type of feed to alert them when someone in their area asks a relevant question. While people in the know will still ask questions to librarians directly, as the network of mobile users becomes larger and larger, the likelihood that individuals will take the time to track down the librarians' contact information drops. This is due to two different aspects of networks: adding nodes to any given network doesn't increase its usefulness linearly, but geometrically; and the information-seeking behavior of connected individuals tends to be peer to peer rather than expert driven.

The network law is known as "Metcalfe's law." Metcalfe's law was originally used to describe the value of a physical network like fax machines, but it is equally applicable to social networks. The law says that "the value of a telecommunications network is proportional to the square of the number of connected users of the system (n2)" (http://en.wikipedia.org/w/index.php?title=Metcalfe%27s_law&oldid=279116371). As more and more users become connected via a mobile handset, their value to their social group as informational nodes increases. The first place people turn for information tends to be people in their family or social circle, so, as these people become more and more connected, it stands to reason that individuals will soon be able to simply ask a question to their network via a conduit like Twitter and expect answers. If libraries want to continue to be a part of the information-seeking process, they will need to be a part of this network, either explicitly (actively friending people who meet specific criteria) or implicitly (monitoring the discussion as noted earlier). The good thing about the increasing size and connectivity of social networks is that, as it becomes easier for patrons to sidestep the library in their seeking of information, the same network makes it easier for libraries to become involved. But libraries need to watch the development of instant and ubiquitous connectivity very closely.

For the academic librarian, instruction will change in the same ways that it is changing across the academy. Instruction is becoming more modular and deliverable via multiple channels. Instruction, especially library instruction, will be delivered both live and recorded, and more and more of it will become a combination of synchronous question and answer and asynchronous lessons. Students will access your instruction virtually in most cases, and they will expect to be able to contact you from the virtual lesson to follow up and ask questions. The "in-class" and "out-of-class" activities will blend in a similar way that reference interactions did such that instructors can expect to be called upon nearly any time.

Librarians can expect their services to move out from behind desks and become localized to the person rather than to a location in the library. They can expect patrons to generally stop approaching the library directly and instead expect the library to be where they are. We need to prepare to embed ourselves into the data stream of the social communications of our patrons.

I hope that this book has given you the information you need to judge both the merits and the possibilities of taking your library into the mobile world. There is a ton of opportunity for libraries in the mobile world, most of which are only partially being exploited currently. The growth of cell phone use, especially smartphones, is completely off the charts. In the next several years, cell phones will be the most popular way of accessing the Internet in the United States. If libraries don't dive in to the mobile world now, we run the risk of losing out on a significant portion of our future patron base.

As with any book on technology, there will be major changes between the time this manuscript is turned in to the printer and the actual shipment of the book. Thus, a companion wiki will provide continuing updates to the content. An ongoing list of resources and information about mobile hardware and software is available at www.delicious.com/griffey/mobilebook. I will update and attempt to keep current this bibliography by adding links to that URL as I find them. I can be reached directly at griffey@gmail.com, or through my Web site, www.jasongriffey.net, if you have questions or would like to follow up with any of the ideas presented in this book.

BIBLIOGRAPHY AND RECOMMENDED READING

"AirPAC." Available: elibrary.wayne.edu:91.

Allen, Robert. "Greetings from Product Development" (February 29, 2008). Available: brewing.iii.com/2008/02/29/greetings-from-product-development.

"Amanda's Mobile Bookmarks on Delicious." Available: delicious.com/amanda/mobile.

Ankeny, Jason. "U.S. Wireless Subscribers Top 270 Million" (April 1, 2009). Available: www.fiercewireless.com/ctialive/story/u-s-wireless-subscribers-top-270-million/2009-04-01?utm_medium=nl&utm_source=internal&cmp-id=EMC-NL-FW&dest=FMC.

AppsAmuck. "iPhone Development Tutorials and Examples." Available: www.appsamuck.com.

Bai, Sheryl, Benjamin Smith, Chris Tonjes, Bill McLendon, and Aaron Schmidt. "CIL2009: Mobile Library Apps" (April 1, 2009). Available: librarianinblack.typepad.com/librarianinblack/2009/04/cil2009-mobile-library-apps.html.

"Baylor University, Crouch Fine Arts Library, AR2G." Available: www.baylor.edu/lib/finearts/index.php?id=30624.

"SMS—Biblioteksvar." Available: biblioteksvar.no/en/sms/.

Bishop, Todd. "Windows Mobile Misses Target" (July 30, 2008). Available: www.seattlepi.com/business/372906_msftmobile31.html.

"Books for the iPod." Thomas Ford Memorial Library. Available: www.fordlibrary.org/booksmoviesmagazinesmore/ipodbooks .html.

"Boopsie." Available: www.boopsie.com.

Brantley, Peter. "A Mobile Read (with White Space)" (September 27, 2008). Available: radar.oreilly.com/archives/2007/09/a-mobile-read-w.html.

Breeding, Marshall. "SMS Offers Libraries New Talk Tool" (2005). Available: www.librarytechnology.org/ltg-displaytext.pl?RC= 11902.

Brownlow, Mark. "Email and Webmail User Statistics" (2008). Available: www.email-marketing-reports.com/metrics/email-statistics.htm.

"Browser Webmonkey" (February11, 2009). Available: www .webmonkey.com/tutorial/Browser-Specific_CSS_Hacks.

"BSU Libraries Mobile." Available: www.bsu.edu/libraries/mobile.

Buchanan, Matt. "Giz Explains: Why Wimax and LTE Wireless 4G Data Will Blow Your Mind" (March 11, 2009). Available: i.gizmodo .com/5168035/giz-explains-why-wimax-and-lte-wireless-4g-data -will-blow-your-mind.

"CiL: SMS in Libraries: The Killer Ap?" (March 24, 2006). Available: www.blogwithoutalibrary.net/181.

"Columbus Metropolitan Library—AquaBrowser Library." Available: catalog.columbuslibrary.org/accessible.ashx.

Coulton, Jonathan. "Jonathan Coulton, Blog Archive, SMS to Email List" (2009). Available: www.jonathancoulton.com/ 2009/03/09/sms-to-email-list.

"CTIA—The Wireless Association" (April 1, 2009). Available: www .ctia.org/media/press/body.cfm/prid/1811.

"The Demon-Haunted World." Available: www.slideshare.net/ blackbeltjones/the-demonhaunted-world.

"Enter a URL: Google Mobile Site Viewer." Available: www.google .com/gwt/n.

Falls, Jason. "The Good and the Bad of Mobile Marketing, Social Media Explorer" (October 10, 2008). Available: www

.socialmediaexplorer.com/2008/10/10/the-good-and-the-bad-of-mobile-marketing.

Goodyear, Dana. "Letter from Japan: I Heart Novels: The New Yorker" (December 22, 2008). Available: www.newyorker.com/reporting/2008/12/22/081222fa_fact_goodyear.

"Google Translate." Available: translate.google.com/translate?hl=en&sl=ja&u=http://company.maho.jp/business/iland.html&prev=/search%3Fq%3Dhttp://company.maho.jp/%26hl%3Den%26sa%3DG.

Gundotra, Vic. "Follow the Mobile User" (March 29, 2009). Available: www.techcrunchit.com/2009/03/29/follow-the-mobile-user.

Hamilton, Matt. "CIL2009: Mobile Practices and Search: What's Hot!" (April 6, 2009). Available: matthewdhamilton.com/wp/2009/04/06/cil2009-mobile-practices-search-what%E2%80%99s-hot.

Heng, Christopher. "How to Use Different CSS Style Sheets for Different Browsers (And How to Hide CSS Code from Older Browsers)" (September 7, 2008). Available: www.thesitewizard.com/css/excludecss.shtml.

Herrman, John. "Giz Explains: All the Smartphone Mobile Apps Stores—Mobile App Stores—Gizmodo" (April 6, 2009). Available: i.gizmodo.com/5199933/giz-explains-all-the-smartphone-mobile-app-stores.

Hossack, John. "The Complete Google Analytics User Guide—VKI Studios Blog" (June 5, 2009). Available: blog.vkistudios.com/index.cfm/2009/6/5/The-Google-Analytics-Power-User-Guide.

"How Many iPhones in the World? Ask Metafilter" (January 14, 2009). Available: ask.metafilter.com/111634/How-many-iPhones-in-the-world.

Ihnatko, Andy. "Andy Ihnatko's Celestial Waste of Bandwidth: The Great Google Phone Brain Dump: Part One" (October 16, 2008). Available: ihnatko.com/index.php/2008/10/16/the-great-google-phone-brain-dump-part-one.

"Innovative Interfaces Debuts AirPac" (July 16, 2001). Available: www.libraryjournal.com/article/CA94780.html.

"Keitai Novels" (May 20, 2009). Available: bit.ly/oqtsU.

King, David Lee. "CIL2009: Handhelds & Mobiles" (April 1, 2009). Available: www.davidleeking.com/2009/04/01/cil2009-handhelds-mobile.

———. "Tinkering in the Techie Toybox—My Presentation" (November 14, 2008). Available: www.davidleeking.com/2008/11/14/tinkering-in-the-techie-toybox-my-presentation.

Kirkpatrick, Marshall. "Layar Could Be the Future of 'Augmented Reality'" (June 16, 2009). Available: www.readwriteweb.com/archives/layar_could_be_the_future_of_augmented_reality.php.

Lentz, Michelle. "The Library in the Cloud" (October 21, 2008). Available: bub.blicio.us/library_cloud_computin.

Levin, Alan. "2009 Horizon Report" (January 25, 2009). Available: www.nmc.org/publications/2009-horizon-report.

"Library Catalog—Mobile Interfaces" (2008). Available: www.flickr.com/photos/users_lib/sets/72157606400611761/.

"Library OPACs & Mobile-Friendly Features" (August 10, 2008). Available: userslib.com/2008/08/10/library-opacs-mobile-friendly-features.

"Library Websites—Mobile Interfaces" (2009). Available: www.flickr.com/photos/users_lib/sets/72157606324688497.

Lipka, Sara. "U. of Michigan Students Use Bluetooth to Help Blind and Seeing Pedestrians Roam Cities" (October 14, 2008). Available: chronicle.com/wiredcampus/index.php?id=3387.

"M-Libraries" (2009). Available: www.libsuccess.org/index.php?title=M-Libraries.

"Maintaining Browser-Specific CSS" (September 26, 2008). Available: ajaxian.com/archives/maintaining-css.

"Make It Mobile" Available: www.iyhy.com.

"Make Your Site Mobile Friendly" (May 14, 2007). Available: carsonified.com/blog/features/css/make-your-site-mobile-friendly/.

"Making a Podcast." Apple. (2009). Available: www.apple.com/itunes/whatson/podcasts/specs.html.

Mawhinney, Bryan. "Google Sync Beta for iPhone, WinMo and SyncML Phones" (February 9, 2009). Available: googlemobile .blogspot.com/2009/02/google-sync-beta-for-iphone-winmo-and .html.

Melanson, Donald. "Object-Based Media Project Brings iPhone and RIFD Together" (April 15, 2009). Available: www.engadget .com/2009/04/15/object-based-media-project-brings-iphone-and-rfid-together/.

"MIT Mobile Web" (2009). Available: mobi.mit.edu/about.

"MIT Mobile Web Open Source Project" (2008). Available: mitmobileweb.sourceforge.net.

"Mobile Clubs." Broadtexter. (2009). Available: www.broadtexter .com.

"Mobile Health and the iPhone" (July 23, 2008). Available: chilmarkresearch.com/2008/07/23/mobile-health-and-the-iphone.

"Mobile Library Catalogs" (September 3, 2008). Available: userslib .com/2008/09/03/mobile-library-catalogs.

"Mobile Mania—Library Websites" (July 23, 2008). Available: userslib.com/2008/07/23/mobile-mania-library-websites.

"Mobile Resources" (2009). Available: www.ocls.info/Virtual/ Galleries/Topical/mobilc.asp?bhcp=1.

"Mobile Services" (2009). Available: www.skokie.lib.il.us/s_about/ mobile_services.asp.

"Mozes." Available: www.mozes.com.

"NEW Libraries Consortium." Available: libraries.etsu.edu/ airpac/jsp/airpacIndex.jsp.

"Novel Cellout" (January 7, 2009). Available: www.metafilter.com/ 78065/novel-cellout.

"OCLS Mobile for iPhone and iTouch." YouTube (March 12, 2009). Available: www.youtube.com/watch?v=991qqTnvqfo.

"Online Reference." Available: www.libsuccess.org/index.php? title=Online_Reference.

"Online Reference" (2009). Available: libsuccess.org/index.php?
title=Online_Reference#Libraries_Offering_SMS_Reference_
Services.

"OnPoint Web Manager." Available: opmobile.com/opwm.

"OSU Library Lab: Mobile Catalog." Ohio State University (April
23, 2009). Available: library.osu.edu/blogs/labs/2009/04/23/
osu-library-labs-mobile-catalog.

"Overview [OCLC—NetLibrary eAudiobooks]" (2009). Available:
www.oclc.org/audiobooks/overview/default.htm.

"Pattie Maes Demos the Sixth Sense." Available: www.ted.com/
index.php/talks/pattie_maes_demos_the_sixth_sense.html.

"Pocket World in Figures: Computer Ownership" (December 18,
2008). Available: www.economist.com/research/articlesBySubject/
displayStory.cfm?story_id=12758865&subjectID=348909&fsrc=
nwl.

"Q: Cell (Mobile) Phone Screen Resolution List." Google Answers.
Available: answers.google.com/answers/threadview?id=439967.

"QR Code." Wikipedia (June 2, 2009). Available: en.wikipedia
.org/wiki/QR_Code.

Restaino, Nicole. "New! Cell Phone Audio Tour of Paley Library"
(March 16, 2009). Available: blog.library.temple.edu/liblog/
archives/2009/03/new-cell-phone.html.

Schmidt, Aaron. "DCPL iPhone App Available" (April 6, 2009).
Available: dclibrarylabs.org/dcpl-iphone-app-code-available.

"Skokie Library Home Page." Available: skokielibrary.info.

"Skokie Public Library" (2009). Available: skokielibrary.info/
mobile.

"Skweezer" (2009). Available: www.skweezer.com.

"SMS." Wikipedia (June 6, 2009). Available: en.wikipedia.org/
wiki/Short_message_service.

"SMS Gateway." Wikipedia (June 16, 2009). Available: en
.wikipedia.org/wiki/SMS_gateway#Carrier-Provided_E-Mail_or_
Web_to_SMS_Gateways.

"SMS Gateway" (2009). Available: www.clickatell.com/products/
sms_gateway.php.

Stross, Randall. "What Carriers Aren't Eager to Tell You about Texting" (December 26, 2008). Available: www.nytimes.com/2008/12/28/business/28digi.html?_r=2.

"Superpatron—Edward Vielmetti Is Mobilizing the Friends of the Library for the Blind" (May 30, 2008). Available: vielmetti.typepad.com/superpatron/2008/05/mobile-versions.html.

"Text a Librarian" (2008). Available: www.textalibrarian.com.

"Text a Librarian" (2009). Available: www.selu.edu/library/askref/text/index.html.

"TextMarks" (2008). Available: www.textmarks.com.

"Text Messaging Reference—Yale Science Libraries" (May 14, 2009). Available: www.library.yale.edu/science/textmsg.html.

Trapani, Gina. "One Dozen Super-Useful (and Free!) Android Apps" (April 15, 2009). Available: lifehacker.com/5212542/one-dozen-super+useful-and-free-android-apps.

"Usablenet Assistive Main Page" (2004). Available: transcoder.usablenet.com/tt.

Vanderbeeken, Mark. "4 Billion Mobile Users by the End of 2008" (September 26, 2008). Available: www.core77.com/blog/technology/4_billion_mobile_phone_users_by_the_end_of_2008_11266.asp.

"VC6096 WWAN In-Vehicle/Fixed Mount Mobile Computer." Available: www.motorola.com/Business/US-EN/Business+Product+and+Services/Mobile+Computers/Vehicle-mounted+Computers/VC6096_Mobile_Computer_US-EN.

"Video Collection." Ann Arbor District Library (2009). Available: www.aadl.org/video/collection.

"Widget Tweaks." LibraryH3lp (May 31, 2009). Available: libraryh3lp.blogspot.com/2009/05/widget-tweaks.html.

"Wireless Application Protocol." Wikipedia (May 25, 2009). Available: en.wikipedia.org/wiki/Wireless_Application_Protocol.

"Yahoo! Placemaker Beta." Yahoo! (2009). Available: developer.yahoo.com/geo/placemaker.

INDEX

Page numbers followed by the letter "f" indicate figures.

ABOUT THE AUTHOR

Jason Griffey is an Assistant Professor and the Head of Library Information Technology at the University of Tennessee at Chattanooga. He graduated with his MLS from the University of North Carolina at Chapel Hill and prior to that did graduate work in philosophy at both Ohio University and the University of Maryland at College Park. His research interests include technology use in higher education, social networks and technology, intellectual property, and other digital issues.

Jason can be found on the Web at www.jasongriffey.net. His blog, Pattern Recognition, where he writes about himself, libraries, technology, and anything that catches his interest, can be found at www.jasongriffey.net/wp. You can find Jason online nearly everywhere, but especially Flickr, Delicious, Twitter, blip.tv, ClaimID, LibraryThing, LinkedIn, Slideshare, and other social networks, all under the username griffey.

Jason was named one of *Library Journal*'s Movers & Shakers for 2009.

He spends his free time with his daughter Eliza, reading, playing games, and preparing for the inevitable zombie apocalypse.